DMN in Action with OpenRules

A Practical Guide for Development of Business Rules and Decision Management Applications using Decision Model and Notation (DMN) Standard and OpenRules

By Jacob Feldman, PhD

ISBN 978-1-5206053-8-8

Table of Contents

Preface

About Business Decision Modeling and DMN. Nowadays Business Decision Modeling is rapidly becoming major technological and methodological framework to support decision making approaches across a wide range of business problems from loan origination and insurance underwriting to clinical guidelines and recommendations. The recently introduced OMG standard "Decision Model and Notation (DMN)" [1] brings standardization to decision modeling, an emerging best practice. Decision Modeling clearly defines a business target, shows how to orchestrate decision management techniques, supports interoperability, and integrates decision models into modern enterprise architectures. DMN quickly becomes a mainstream approach supported by many Business Rules and Decision Management tools [6].

To Whom This Guide Is Oriented. This guide is oriented to people who want to build operational decision models for their own business environments. They've probably already looked at the DMN standard itself and quickly figured out that the text of the standard is more oriented to DMN vendors (implementers) than to practitioners. They've probably read or at least navigated through recently published DMN textbooks like [2]-[4], which are trying to cover all (!) DMN aspects and to provide methodological recommendations for how to apply DMN in the real-world decision modeling.

Thus, we expect that our readers are already convinced of the value of the decision modeling proposition. However, they still have problems with understanding what actually should be done to build their own operational decision models.

How Readers Create Executable Decision Models. The objective of this guide is to help readers quickly learn how to apply the DMN approach to build working decision models. To achieve this objective, this book will guide readers on how to create working decision models for simple and complex business problems. More importantly, readers should be able to execute (!) their decision models and integrate them into their own IT systems. That's why we called this guide "DMN in Action"!

While DMN is supposed to take care of future interoperability (tool independence), a reader needs to choose concrete DMN tools to actually create and execute decision models. Without using such tools it's simply impossible to achieve our objective. So, as readers go through this guide, they can utilize the following tools:

1) Microsoft Excel: without doubt the most popular tool among business analysts in any industry. Our readers will mainly use Excel as the best table editor to create and enhance business decision models.
2) OpenRules: a highly popular open source business rules and decision management system. Our readers will use OpenRules to test (that assumes an ability to execute!) their decision models.

The website www.DmnInAction.com offers a reader two options: 1) open, analyze, and execute all decision models online without any download; 2) install a free evaluation version of OpenRules and analyze/modify/execute all provided or your own decision models.

Instead of Excel a reader may use Google Docs or Open Office. If a reader prefers to use a DMN implementation [6] different from OpenRules, they still can do it, but the described DMN constructs need to be adjusted to the tool-specific DMN representations.

How this Guide Is Written. This guide was written in style of dialog between the AUTHOR and the READER. The guide consists of multiple dialog-sessions, during which AUTHOR and READER are trying to build concrete decision models. They are freely discussing why and how they are actually building decision models, without avoiding any of the missteps, pitfalls, and alternative approaches.

From one decision model to another the AUTHOR will lead the inquisitive and receptive READER to different decision modeling concepts and notions emphasizing and/or demystifying especially complicated aspects, and attracting the reader's attention to special situations that occur in the real-world decision modeling.

About the Reader. We consider the READER to be a subject matter expert or a business analyst without any programming experience. He or she may be proficient in Excel but more importantly is a person who really wants to understand how to build good decision models that can be adjusted and enhanced over time as business conditions change.

Only once, in the Dialog-Session 3, will the READER be joined by the DEVELOPER, who also will be "inquisitive and receptive" but from a purely IT integration perspective.

The actual reader of this guide will find this text to be perhaps more like a freely told story or, rather a freely conducted discussion. Being represented by a fictional READER, the actual reader will hopefully find the answers to a lot of his/her own questions, and will eventually gain an intrinsic understanding of the DMN-based decision modeling technique.

About the Author. The fictional AUTHOR in this guide represents me, Jacob Feldman, the Chief Technology Officer of the OpenRules, Inc., a US corporation that created and maintains the open source Business Rules and Decision Management system commonly known simply as "OpenRules" [5]. Over the course of dialog-sessions I will try to share my multi-year experience as a decision modeling practitioner who has helped our customers develop and maintain production-quality decision models in various business domains.

I want to warn the readers that this guide by no means is a DMN textbook as it does not cover all the items introduced in the DMN standard. On the contrary, it concentrates on the most frequently used decision modeling constructs described in DMN and uses their particular implementations in the OpenRules formats.

As the AUTHOR, I took a liberty of choosing the DMN concepts that are most frequently used and helpful and those which should be avoided. I simply don't mention some concepts currently included in the DMN standard which I do not recommend for use. In particular, the AUTHOR will not talk about hit policies with priorities or about pure programming constructs such as loops or if-then-else statements included in the DMN Friendly Enough Expression Language (FEEL). As the AUTHOR, I promised the READER to stay away from programming, and I will try to stick to this promise over the course of all (well, almost all) dialog-sessions. At the same time, the READER and I will actively use the FEEL syntax to represent various business expressions and calculation formulas.

The nice thing about the DMN standard is that it allows vendors to compete on different representations of the same DMN concepts as long as they have the same semantic meaning. The reader may find that OpenRules graphical representations of some DMN concepts are slightly different from examples included in the current DMN specification. For instance, we do not use single-character and double-character abbreviations for hit policies which are supposed to be placed into a separate cell of every decision table. Instead, we use keywords such as "DecisionTableSingleHit" or "DecisionTableMultiHit" in decision table titles.

Finally, I believe it is extremely important to keep this guide as small as possible (no more than 150 pages) and to allow the reader to start developing their own decision models ASAP. They can do this right after going through the first 3-4 dialog-sessions and actually modifying and executing the provided examples of decision models. In general, the guide provides many examples that can be used as working prototypes. Learning by example is the quickest and easiest way to learn fundamental decision modeling concepts.

How to Use this Guide. It is not necessary to read the entire guide. Even if you read only the first two dialog-sessions, you will get a good introduction to practical decision modeling techniques. The third dialog-session "Integration with IT" allows you to invoke your IT colleagues to make sure that your future real decision models will be as easily integrated into your specific IT infrastructure as it is explained in the guide using a simple example.

Each dialog-session starts with a list of the discussed topics, and you may skip sessions that are of no interest to you. So, you can read dialog-sessions in the presented order, or you may read them in accordance with your actual interest and needs.

What is really important is not just to go through the printed examples but also download, analyze, and execute the described decision models using the supporting software. It will allow you to look at all implementation details directly in Excel including the use of dropdown lists, data validation, cell merging, outlines, and other well-known and very helpful Excel constructs. All figures may also be seen directly in Excel by downloading the related projects from www.DmnInAction.com.

Supporting Software. This guide comes with the software that includes all described decision models in Excel format. To do this, visit www.DmnInAction.com website and you will be able to download them from the page "Decision Models". You also may open OpenRules Why-Analyzer to select, analyze, and test all these decision models online without any downloads or installations.

If you want to download these decision models to your own computer and modify and execute them locally, you may receive the supporting software for free by submitting a request to OpenRules. Alternatively, you may get an evaluation copy directly from www.OpenRules.com and use it to run the existing or to create your own decision models.

I recommend you to check www.DmnInAction.com from time to time as it is being constantly updated with new decision models not described in this guide (yet).

Acknowledgments. First of all, I want to thank the subject experts with whom I was fortunate enough to work developing complex business rules, optimization and machine learning applications over the last two decades. Secondly, I want to thank all the people who helped to bring the DMN standard to the everyday reality for many decision management practitioners worldwide. It would not have happened without previous work and the current support by key architects and actual developers of various business rules and decision management products. Special thanks should go to the authors of the "big" books that together provide methodological guidance for business decision modeling techniques in general and the DMN standard in particular.

And finally, I want to share a little story about people who had no direct acquaintance with modern decision modeling techniques but who essentially incentivized me to write this guide. Many years ago, preparing for my university entrance exams, I read a math book simply known at that time among Soviet high school students as "Tarasov and Tarasova" (by the last name of the authors). The book was written in a very unusual style of dialogs between TEACHER and STUDENT. It was a really enlightening guide that not only demystified complex mathematical concepts but gave me an initial feeling of the beauty and intrinsic integrity of mathematics in general. Thank you, Tarasov & Tarasova!

Jacob Feldman, PhD
Monroe, New Jersey
February 2017

Dialog-Session 1: Introducing Major Concepts by Building an Executable Decision Model

Discussed Topics:

- Decision Requirement Diagram (DRD)
- Tabular Decisions and Sub-Decisions
- Rules Repository
- Decision Tables
- Glossary
- Test Cases
- Executing Decision Model
- Implementation Steps

Related OpenRules Projects:

- DecisionHello
- DecisionHelloWorld

AUTHOR. Hi again. You told me that you've already had a chance to look at the DMN standard, and even looked through several of the latest decision modeling books. Now you want to start building actual decision models.

READER. Yes, and I already understand that DMN and supporting tools may help me to build decision models. However, I have difficulty grasping exactly what decision models are and how I can create workable models myself.

AUTHOR. Many business analysts or subject matter experts who start working with DMN initially face the same issue. I believe the best solution is to create a decision model that you can "touch", execute and analyze. Today we'll specify and build a relatively simple but complete decision model that demonstrates major decision modeling constructs. You will be able not only create a decision model but also to test it using your own test cases and to evaluate the produced results.

READER. I'd like to "touch" a decision model.

AUTHOR. I hope you will at the end of this session. We will start with our own version of "Hello World", that is traditionally the first program people create when they learn a new programming language.

READER. But during our preliminary discussion, you said DMN is oriented to business people like me and you do not plan to teach me any programming language.

AUTHOR. Right, and we will stay away from programming. First, we will define a simple business problem, which I call "Greeting a Customer". Let's assume that our future decision model should produce a greeting like *"Good Afternoon, Mrs. Robinson!"* based on the current time of the day and some information about the customer. For example, such a decision model can be used by an IVR system...

READER. What is IVR?

AUTHOR. You usually deal with an **I**nteractive **V**oice **R**esponse (IVR) system when you call to any customer support and a nice voice asks you to push "hundreds" of buttons before you can reach a live agent.

READER. I hate those systems.

AUTHOR. Me too. Anyway, the first thing that any good interactive system should do is to greet you properly as a valuable customer. The Fig. 1-1 shows different variations of possible greetings:

Dialog-Session 1

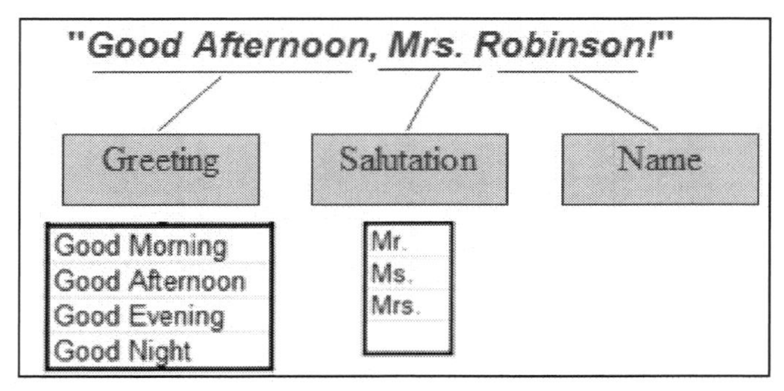

Fig. 1-1

We may assume that "Name" and other related information about the customer is already known. What we want is to automatically define is a Greeting (one out of 4 alternatives) and Salutation (one out of 3 alternatives).

READER. It looks quite simple: we can choose a Greeting based on the time of the day and we can choose a Salutation based on the customer's gender.

AUTHOR. In the real IVR system even this "simple" problem may become much more complex, but let's move forward with what you just said. So, we want to build a decision model capable of producing greetings similar to those in Fig. 1-1 based on some information about the customer. First of all, I suggest giving our decision model a name, e.g. "DetermineCustomerGreeting".

READER. Why did you omit spaces between these 3 words?

AUTHOR. Besides humans who create and maintain this decision model, this name will also be used by an information system that will invoke (execute) our decision model. So, let's consider the absence of spaces as our convention.

READER. OK. One more question: should the names of other decision models start with the word “Determine”?

AUTHOR. Not at all, it is your choice. At the same time, it is a good practice to name your decision model in accordance with what it actually does, e.g. later on we plan to consider decision models “DeterminePatient Therapy”, “CalculateTaxReturn”, “DefineLoanEligibility”, etc. OK, let’s start building our first decision model.

READER. I think we should create decision tables that define our Greeting and Salutation words.

AUTHOR. Quite good, you better call them not “words” but rather decision variables. The decision tables usually specify the decision logic or the “HOW” of your decision model. However, it’s always better to start with an answer to the question “WHAT” that shows the structure of our future decision model. For example, from looking at the Fig. 1-1 it is only natural to conclude that our decision “DetermineCustomerGreeting” consists of two sub-decisions “DefineGreeting” and “DefineSalutation”, and these sub-decisions can be defined using the proper decision tables.

DMN recommends starting with creation of a so called “Decision Requirement Diagram” or DRD. We can do it with any generic diagramming tool such as Visio [Vizio] and a specialized tool such a Decisions First [DFM]. However, I promised you that our main tool over this course will be Excel. Using basic Excel “Insert+Shapes”, I can rather quickly create the first DRD for our decision model. It is presented on Fig. 1-2:

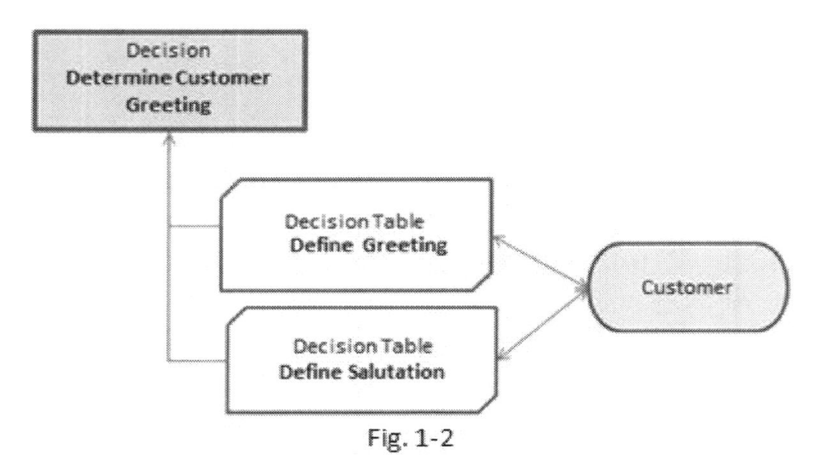

Fig. 1-2

This diagram tells us that to "DetermineCustomerGreeting" we need to "DefineGreeting" and to "DefineSalutation". We also specified a business object "Customer" that provides information for these two decision tables.

In Excel, it is easy to add a hyperlink to each element of the diagram to open to the proper file/table when you click on this element. It makes the DRD a very convenient navigation tool.

READER. Probably DRDs will be useful for more complex decision model, but for such a simple case as ours, this picture probably is not necessary.

AUTHOR. In real world, DRD is useful not only to give a generic view of the decision model, but also to serve as a glue that puts different decision tables together and allows an underlying decision engine to execute our decision models. As Bruce Silver wrote, *"Decision logic is verifiable and executable. What you draw is what you execute"* [3]

To make the DRD on Fig. 1-2 executable, OpenRules allows you to present it in the equivalent tabular format:

Decision DetermineCustomerGreeting	
Decisions	Execute Decision Tables
Define Greeting Variable	DefineGreeting
Define Salutation Variable	DefineSalutation

Fig. 1-3

This is an example of an OpenRules table of the type "Decision" that starts with the proper keyword at the left top corner followed by the name of the table, in this case "DetermineCustomerGreeting". The first column contains descriptions of sub-decisions in plain English (spaces are allowed), and the second column contains the actual names of tables that implement these sub-decisions (no spaces).

READER. Do I always have to specify both a diagram and the equivalent table "Decision"?

AUTHOR. No. To execute your decision model with OpenRules it is enough to define only its tabular format "Decision". However, we are working with several diagraming tool vendors on an integration that will allow our users to automatically generate tables of the type "Decision" directly from the DRDs.

When we define the structure of our decision model, we can describe the actual business logic by creating two decision tables: "DefineGreeting" and "DefineSalutation". Let me create the first table and you will create the second one.

READER. OK. I've seen that you placed the DRD and our table "DetermineCustomerGreeting" in the Excel file "Decision.xls". Will we create these two tables in the same file?

AUTHOR. We can use the same file and different Excel worksheets. However, within real-world decision models people place different decision modeling constructs in different files and even in different folders to simplify future maintenance of their decision models. OpenRules standard examples usually place the standard decision model in the so called "Rules Repository" that in many cases looks as on Fig. 1-4.

I've already created the folder "DecisionHello" as a placeholder for our decision model based on the standard project template provided by OpenRules. It contains folders and files similar to those described on Fig. 1-4.

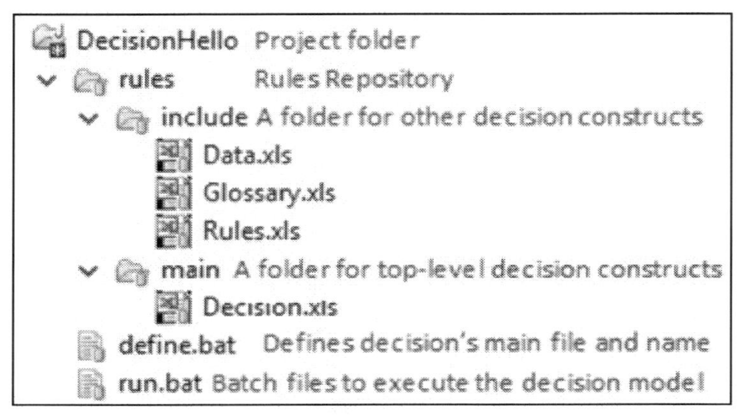

Fig. 1-4

READER. OK, I guess we will talk about files "Glossary.xls" and "Data.xls" later on. For now we will create our decision tables inside the file "Rules.xls".

AUTHOR. Right. First, I will show you how to create a very simple decision table "Define Greeting" in Excel. After a few regular Excel manipulations, I created the following table (again utilizing some OpenRules examples):

	A	B	C	D
1				
2		DecisionTable DefineGreeting		
3		If	Then	
4		Current Hour	Greeting	
5		[0..11)	Good Morning	
6		[11..17)	Good Afternoon	
7		[17..22)	Good Evening	
8		[22-24]	Good Night	
9				

Fig. 1-5

Hopefully this decision table is self-explanatory. Could you try to explain how it is supposed to work?

READER. Yes, it looks quite intuitive to me. There are 4 rules:

1. If Current Hour is between 0 and 11, the Greeting is "Good Morning"
2. If Current Hour is between 11 and 17, the Greeting is "Good Afternoon".
3. If Current Hour is between 17 and 122, the Greeting is "Good Evening".
4. If Current Hour is between 22 and 24, the Greeting is "Good Night".

AUTHOR. The first column is a condition specified by the OpenRules keyword "If", and the second column is a conclusion specified by the keyword "Then". Could you tell me what Greeting will be produced when Current Hour is exactly 11?

READER. "Good Afternoon" because the first interval [0..11) does not include 11 while the second interval [11..17) does.

AUTHOR. Good that you remember this basic math convention from your college years. By the way, instead of [0..11) you also may write:

```
< 11
Less than 11
More or equal 0 and less than 11
```

READER. It's nice. I noticed that you merged columns in the very first "black" row. Why was it necessary?

AUTHOR. To help OpenRules to recognize the table bounds. If I would not merge the columns B and C in the Excel's row 2, OpenRules would "think" that this table has only one column (B). Have you noticed that I also left empty cells around the table?

READER. Probably you did it for esthetic considerations similar to your use of different colors.

AUTHOR. Yes and no. This particular table will work fine even if you don't surround it with empty cells. However, if we have several tables inside the same worksheet, these tables should not touch each other. Even if you want to put some comments near some rows or columns of the decision table, make sure they do not touch the table. By the way, you may insert Excel's own comments anywhere – OpenRules will ignore them, but it will help other people who will analyze your decision table.

READER. How about colors and border shapes? I've seen how precise you were making sure that a separator between columns "If" and "Then" is double-lined.

AUTHOR. Text and background colors, fonts, borders, and other visual elements are used just for consistency and standardization. For example, many OpenRules customers have for years preferred to use a black background and a white foreground in the very first "signature" row. However, some customers prefer other coloring conventions. Contrary to "merging", it does not carry any semantic meaning for OpenRules. Coloring conditions in blue and conclusions in purple comes from the DMN samples as well as a doubled line used to separate conditions and conclusions. Unfortunately, the current version of DMN in certain situations gives semantic meanings to italics and underlining – we, at OpenRules, believe this is a mistake and do not support such interpretations.

READER. Now it is my turn to create a similar decision table "DefineSalutation". I will simply copy/paste your worksheet "DefineGreeting" and will do some refactoring. OK, here is my version:

DecisionTable DefineSalutation	
If	Then
Gender	**Salutation**
Male	Mr.
Female	Mrs.
Female	Ms.

Fig. 1-6

Oops! I need somehow to differentiate between "Mrs." and "Ms." May I add another column with the customer's Marital Status?

AUTHOR. Of course, just insert another column before the column "Then" as you usually do in Excel.

READER. OK, this is simple... But can I simply use the word "Marital Status" as a title of my inserted column?

AUTHOR. Why not? We did not ask anybody's permission when we used the words "Current Hour" or "Gender". It will become another decision variable of our decision model.

READER. Here it goes:

DecisionTable DefineSalutation		
If	If	Then
Gender	Marital Status	Salutation
Male		Mr.
Female	Married	Mrs.
Female	Single	Ms.

Fig. 1-7

AUTHOR. Very good. This is a well-designed decision table. Can you explain why you left Marital Status empty for the first rule?

READER. Because whether Marital Status is "Married" or "Single" the Male's salutation is always "Mr."

AUTHOR. That's right. Just keep in mind that DMN requires in such cases to use a hyphen instead of an empty cell. However, OpenRules correctly interprets both a hyphen and an empty cell.

I want to make a few more comments about the organization of decision tables at Fig. 1-5 and Fig. 1-7. Instead of retyping the same values like Male or Female you may take advantage of Excel's ranges. For example, you may select 3 cells with values

Male, Female, Female in the first column on Fig. 1-7, and then click on the menu-item Data+Data Validation and fill out the displayed dialog as on Fig. 1-8:

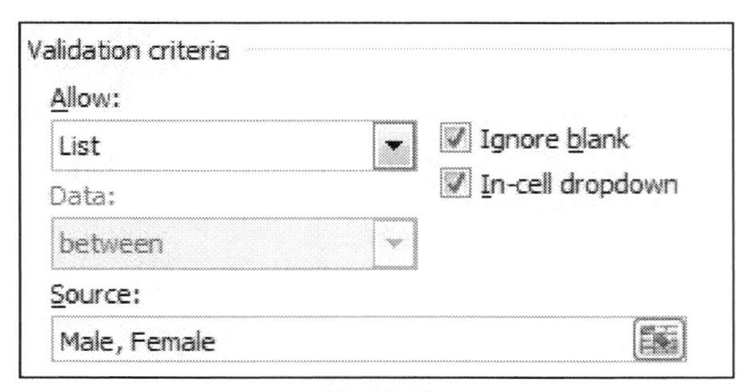

Fig. 1-8

Now you will be able to choose a value from the dropdown list. It makes sense to similarly define dropdown lists for Marital Status, Salutation and Greeting columns.

READER. Of course I know how to use ranges in Excel, but here it really adds value to the design of our decision tables. It is probably especially useful when we have much larger lists of possible values.

AUTHOR. Yes, and later on I will show you how to organize and reuse standard value lists using OpenRules Data tables. Now I want to show you another design of the decision table "Define Salutation":

DecisionTable DefineSalutation					
Condition		Condition		Conclusion	
Gender		Marital Status		Salutation	
Is	Male			Is	Mr.
Is	Female	Is	Married	Is	Mrs.
Is	Female	Is	Single	Is	Ms.

Fig. 1-9

As you can see, I've added special sub-columns for operators "Is" to each table column. I also changed keywords "If" and "Then" to "Condition" and "Conclusion" (they are placed in the merged cells now). While this decision table design may look a little bit more complex, it makes the table more readable when it utilizes different operators like "Is" or "=", "Is Not", "Less", "More or Equal", "Include", "Exclude", and many others. This decision table design was recommended in [7].

READER. I really like this design, even more than the one on Fig. 1-7. Can I use columns of the type "Condition" with two sub-columns for conditions, and columns of the type "Then" for conclusions?

AUTHOR. Yes, you can mix them in the way you want. By the way you can use the keyword "Action" as a synonym for "Then". Now it's time to finalize our decision model.

READER. I thought we had already defined the business logic.

AUTHOR. Yes, but to be able to test (execute) our decision model, we also need to define a business glossary and test cases. Let's start with a glossary that will list all our decision variables categorized by the business concepts they belong to.

In our case it is quite simple because we use only the following decision variables:

- **Current Hour**
- **Greeting**
- **Gender**
- **Marital Status**
- **Salutation.**

Obviously, variables Gender and Marital Status belong to a business concept that we may call "Customer". Do variables Current Hour, Greeting and Salutation also belong to a Customer?

READER. We may assume so... On the other hand, Current Hour depends on the location from where the customer is calling.

AUTHOR. We will deal with these considerations later on – now I want us to finalize and to execute our decision model ASAP. Here is the simplest glossary table for our decision model (I placed it into the file rules/include/Glossary.xls):

Glossary glossary		
Variable	**Business Concept**	**Attribute**
Gender	Customer	gender
Marital Status		maritalStatus
Current Hour		currentHour
Greeting		greeting
Salutation		salutation

Fig. 1-10

I copied and pasted all 5 decision variables from our decision tables to the first column. As we agreed, they all belong to the business concept "Customer" defined in the merged second column. OpenRules also requires us to provide technical names (or attributes) for every decision variable in the third column. These names do not allow spaces and will be used in the future to integrate our decision model with an actual IT system.

READER. Should I always start these technical names with a small letter and then use capital letters for all consecutive words?

AUTHOR. It's better to follow this, so-called "Camel" naming convention as in real-world applications these attributes will correspond the underlying Java objects – but you do not have to worry about this.

Now we should define test cases. As we planned (see Fig. 1-4 above), I will place them to the file" rules/include/Data.xls".

READER. I guess we simply should define several customers with variables Gender, Marital Status, and Current Hour already defined. Then during the testing our decision model will produce the proper values for Greeting and Salutation.

AUTHOR. That's right. OpenRules offers you a quite powerful while simple mechanism known as "Test Harness". Everything is defined in special Excel tables. First we define a so-called Datatype table for our business concept Customer:

Datatype Customer	
String	gender
String	maritalStatus
int	currentHour
String	greeting
String	salutation

Fig. 1-11

This table starts with the keyword "Datatype" following the name of the datatype after a space – in this case "Datatype Customer". Then we list different attributes. The first column contains attribute types, e.g. "String" for text variables, "int" for integer variables, "double" for real variables, "Date" for dates. The second column contains the names of attributes exactly as they were defined in our Glossary in Fig. 1-10.

READER. I guest capitalization is important here.

AUTHOR. Yes, very important. If you write "string" instead of "String" or "Int" instead of "int", OpenRules will point you to a syntax error "Unknown type" (indicating the exact cell where this error occurred). Now let's create test customers using the following table of the type "Data":

Data Customer customers				
gender	maritalStatus	currentHour	greeting	salutation
Gender	Marital Status	Current Hour	Greeting	Salutation
Female	Married	20	?	?
Male	Single	11	?	?

Fig. 1-12

This table starts with the keyword "Data" following the datatype and the name of the array of customers – in this case "Data Customer customers". The second row contains the technical names of Customer's attributes, and the third column contains the business names. The business names are usually the names of variables but you can use any name as the technical names already provide mapping to the decision variables from the glossary. Then we may define as many rows as we want to specify particular customers.

READER. I got it. Do we always have to put '?' for unknown variables?
AUTHOR. In this case you may leave these cells empty, but for integer or double variables you need to put in some initial values (e.g. -1) that indicate that these variables are not defined yet.

OpenRules also allows you to define the expected results for each test case. Then it automatically checks if the actual results correspond to the expected results and shows mismatches. Here is the proper table of the type "DecisionTableTest":

DecisionTableTest testCases			
#	ActionUseObject	ActionExpect	ActionExpect
Test ID	Customer	Greeting	Salutation
Test 1	:= customers[0]	Good Evening	Mrs.
Test 2	:= customers[1]	Good Afternoon	Mr.

Fig. 1-13

The name "testCases" is the name used by the default test launcher. Each test has its own ID defined in the first column of the type "#". This table can use different business objects (concepts) defined in the column of the type "ActionUseObject" – in this case we have only one object "Customer". We also can add different expected test results using the columns of the type "ActionExpect" and the corresponding variable names (like Greeting and Salutation).

READER. I can see that the first test customer is expected to generate Greeting "Good Afternoon" and Salutation "Mrs." But I am a little bit confused with this strange formula:

:= customers[0]

AUTHOR. I agree that it may look confusing for a beginner. The real reason is that this is an example of a Java snippet that OpenRules allows you to put in any cell of your OpenRules table. The sign ":=" indicates that this is a Java snippet (expression) and the index [0] indicates that you want to use the very first element of the array "customers" defined on Fig. 12. In Java, the array indexation always starts with 0.

READER. But you promised to keep me away from programming and now we talk about Java...

AUTHOR. Sorry, but this is how the optional (!) Test Harness is currently implemented. You don't really have to know that this is an actual Java snippet -- simply follow this convention when you define test objects. However, in real-world decision models sometimes you would like to invoke predefined Java methods, and it is not so bad to know that OpenRules provides this capability by using ":=".

READER. I'd rather not have the expected values at all and not have to deal with these Java details.

AUTHOR. It may be true for this, very simple decision model. There is a way to execute all test cases directly from the array "customers" and then visually compare the results with what you expected. However, the Test Harness is very important for real-world decision modeling. We do have customers who maintain decision models with thousands of decision tables. Along with a large rule repository, they also maintain a test repository with thousands of test cases, all of which contain the expected results. When they make changes to the rule repository, they always run Test Harness to make sure that new changes did not spoil already tested results. It is simply impossible to do it manually. This approach is called "***Test-Driven Decision Modeling***"!

READER. OK, I got it. The use of ":=" is not a big price to pay for this functionality. Are we now ready to run these test cases?

AUTHOR. Only one more thing is required. We need to explicitly tell OpenRules which business objects correspond to business concepts defined in the Glossary. It can be done using the following table of type "DecisionObject" (I recommend keeping it in the file Decision.xls):

DecisionObject decisionObjects	
Business Concept	Business Object
Customer	:= decision.get("Customer")

Fig. 1-14

Yes, here we are again using a Java snippet

:= decision.get("Customer")

However, your IT colleagues would really appreciate this capability as it dramatically simplifies the future integration of your tested decision model with their actual business objects that will be used in the production environment.

And finally, we should specify the names for our main file Decision.xls (FILE_NAME) and our main decision name from the table "Decision" (DECISION_NAME). These names are defined in the file "DecisionHello/**define.bat**" contains as follows:

```
set FILE_NAME=rules/main/Decision.xls
set DECISION_NAME=DetermineCustomerGreeting
```

Now you are able to execute your decision model against our test cases. Simply double-click on the file "**run.bat**" that is located in the same folder "DecisionHello".

READER. Finally! Wow, it ran really fast. Here are the results:

```
*** Decision DetermineCustomerGreeting ***
Decision has been initialized

RUN TEST: Test 1
Decision Run has been initialized
Decision DetermineCustomerGreeting: Define
Greeting Word
Assign: Greeting = Good Evening [Good Evening]
Decision DetermineCustomerGreeting: Define
Salutation Word
Conclusion: Salutation Is Mrs. [Mrs.]
Decision has been finalized
Validating results for the test <Test 1>
Test 1 was successful

RUN TEST: Test 2
Decision Run has been initialized
Decision DetermineCustomerGreeting: Define
Greeting Word
Assign: Greeting = Good Afternoon [Good Afternoon]
Decision DetermineCustomerGreeting: Define
Salutation Word
Conclusion: Salutation Is Mr. [Mr.]
Decision has been finalized
Validating results for the test <Test 2>
Test 2 was successful
All 2 tests succeeded!
```

Fig. 1-15

AUTHOR. This is the execution protocol of your testing. It shows execution steps and results for each Test Run.

READER. I see that first OpenRules executed our sub-decision "Define Greeting Word" and our decision table assigned "Good Evening" to the variable Greeting. Then the second decision table made a Conclusion: `Salutation Is Mrs.` This is exactly what was expected. And we got similar results for the second test. Can I add another test-customer?

AUTHOR. Be my guest.

READER. OK, I've just added the third test customer who is a single female that calls at 22:00:

Data Customer customers				
gender	maritalStatus	currentHour	greeting	salutation
Gender	Marital Status	Current Hour	Greeting	Salutation
Female	Married	20	?	?
Male	Single	11	?	?
Female	Single	22	?	?

DecisionTableTest testCases			
#	ActionUseObject	ActionExpect	ActionExpect
Test ID	Customer	Greeting	Salutation
Test 1	:= customers[0]	Good Evening	Mrs.
Test 2	:= customers[1]	Good Afternoon	Mr.
Test 3	:= customers[2]	Good Afternoon	Mrs.

Fig. 1-16

Let me run test-cases again:

```
RUN TEST: Test 3
Decision Run has been initialized
Decision DetermineCustomerGreeting: Define Greeting
Word
Assign: Greeting = Good Night [Good Night]
Decision DetermineCustomerGreeting: Define
Salutation Word
Conclusion: Salutation Is Ms. [Ms.]
Decision has been finalized
Validating results for the test <Test 3>
MISMATCH: variable 'Greeting' has value 'Good Night'
while 'Good Afternoon' was expected
MISMATCH: variable 'Salutation' has value 'Ms.'
while 'Mrs.' was expected
Test 3 was unsuccessful
```

Fig. 1-17

Note that I intentionally made errors in the expected Greeting and Salutation. As a result, we received two mismatches which I just highlighted. It seems I really can "touch" our decision model.

AUTHOR. Congratulations! Now I can say that you got the first taste of how to build a decision model using OpenRules-based DMN implementation.

Let's summarize our **major implementation steps**:

1. **Create DRD** (Decision Requirement Diagram) and its tabular representations of the type "Decision" - Figures 2 and 3
2. **Create Decision Tables** – Figures 1-6 and 1-9
3. **Create Glossary** – Fig. 1-10
4. **Create Test Cases** – Fig. 1-16
5. **Executed Test Cases** – Figures 1-15 and 1-17.

While we used these five steps for a simple decision model, they represent a quite generic implementation schema for much more complex decision models as well.

Dialog-Session 2: Enhancing Decision Model "Determine Customer Greeting"

Discussed Topics:

Adding New Decision Variables
Single-Hit Decision Tables
Comparing Dates
Commenting Out Unused Tables
Importance of Testing

Related OpenRules Project:

DecisionHelloWithDates

AUTHOR. Usually the first working decision model is just a good starting point and business people continue to enhance their decisions by adding more concepts and related decision logic. During this session we also will try to enhance our decision model "DecisionHello" to show new DMN capabilities while making it look closer to real-world decision models.

READER. Good, because when I am thinking about decision models we want to use in my organization, they would have many more decision variables, and the decision tables would need to cover many exceptions.

AUTHOR. OK, but we will add some enhancements one by one making sure that our model keeps working. First, I want our model to make exceptions for young customers by producing greetings like "**Good Afternoon, Young Robinson!**"

READER. While I think it is not right to mess with somebody's age, let's do it as an example. First, we probably need to define "young customers".

AUTHOR. Let's say they should be 7 years old or younger.

READER. In this case we just need to add one more condition to the decision table "DefineSalutation". It should check if the customer's Age is less than 8.

AUTHOR. Sounds good. Do you want to try to make the proper changes?

READER. No problem. Assuming that we will define the variable "Age", I will simply add one more rule at the end of this table – see my new table on Fig. 2-1:

DecisionTable DefineSalutation							
Condition		Condition		Condition		Conclusion	
Gender		Marital Status		Age		Salutation	
Is	Male					Is	Mr.
Is	Female	Is	Married			Is	Mrs.
Is	Female	Is	Single			Is	Ms.
Is				<	8	Is	Young

Fig. 2-1

AUTHOR. Adding a new column "Age" so quickly, shows you really have a good grasp of Excel. Now, could you explain how this decision table will work for a male customer of the age 5?

READER. Easy... Wait a second! Do you want to tell me that the first rule will be satisfied and the produced Salutation will be "Mr'" and not "Young"?

AUTHOR. Yes, it will. And the actual reason is that by default our decision table is **single-hit** as specified by the keyword "DecisionTable".

READER. Single-hit? What does it exactly mean?

AUTHOR. It means that when the first rule (counting from top-down) is satisfied, its conclusions will be executed and all remaining rules will be ignored.

READER. WOW! I could have expected that the decision table behaves this way. What if I add the condition "Age >= 8" to the first 3 rules?

AUTHOR. This will fix the problem. Just for your information, there are other types of decision tables, such as multiple-hit decision tables. But we will talk about them during the future sessions. By the way, you may merge the same operations and values to make your table look better.

READER. OK, here is a new version:

DecisionTable DefineSalutation							
Condition		Condition		Condition		Conclusion	
Gender		Marital Status		Age		Salutation	
Is	Male					Is	Mr.
Is	Female	Is	Married	>=	8	Is	Mrs.
Is	Female	Is	Single			Is	Ms.
				<	8	Is	Young

Fig. 2-2

AUTHOR. Looks good. By the way, instead of the operator "<" you may write "Is Less" and instead of the operator ">=" you may write "Is More Or Equal". Now, what we should do to test your new decision table?

READER. We need to add the variable Age to our glossary. Here is the modified glossary will look like:

Glossary glossary		
Variable	**Business Concept**	**Attribute**
Gender	Customer	gender
Marital Status		maritalStatus
Age		age
Current Hour		currentHour
Greeting		greeting
Salutation		salutation

Fig. 2-3

AUTHOR. How about test cases?

READER. Of course. First I need to add "age" to the Datatype:

Datatype Customer	
String	gender
String	maritalStatus
int	age
int	currentHour
String	greeting
String	salutation

Fig. 2.4

And here is the Data table "customers" with an additional column for "Age":

Data Customer customers					
gender	maritalStatus	currentHour	greeting	salutation	age
Gender	**Marital Status**	**Current Hour**	**Greeting**	**Salutation**	**Age**
Female	Married	20	?	?	45
Male	Single	11	?	?	20
Female	Single	15	?	?	5

Fig. 2-5

AUTHOR. Very good. I noticed that you correctly made sure that the first "black" row is correctly merged covering a new row as well.

READER. I've also corrected the expected results in the table "testCases":

DecisionTableTest testCases			
#	ActionUseObject	ActionExpect	ActionExpect
Test ID	**Customer**	**Greeting**	**Salutation**
Test 1	:= customers[0]	Good Evening	Mrs.
Test 2	:= customers[1]	Good Afternoon	Mr.
Test 3	:= customers[2]	Good Afternoon	Young

Fig. 2-6

The third case should produce the salutation "Young". Correct?

AUTHOR. Double-click on "run.bat" and we will see.

READER. Yes, we got Salutation Young in the third test case, and the first two cases are also correct:

```
RUN TEST: Test 3
Decision Run has been initialized
Decision DetermineCustomerGreeting: Define
Greeting Word
Greeting := Good Afternoon
Decision DetermineCustomerGreeting: Define
Salutation Word
Conclusion: Salutation Is Young
Decision has been finalized
Validating results for the test <Test 3>
Test 3 was successful
All 3 tests succeeded!
```

Fig. 2-7

AUTHOR. Good. What if we want to produce the salutation "Young" only for boys?

READER. I will simply add a check for Male in the last rule of the table "DefineSalutation".

AUTHOR. In this case what will happen when a customer is a 7 years old female?

READER. You are right -- no rules will be satisfied and the Salutation will remain undefined. Should I add one more rule (the default) to explicitly assign '?' to Salutation?

AUTHOR. It certainly will be better than "do nothing"...

READER. OK. Here is my updated decision table:

DecisionTable DefineSalutation							
Condition		Condition		Condition		Conclusion	
Gender		Marital Status		Age		Salutation	
Is	Male					Is	Mr.
Is	Female	Is	Married	>=	8	Is	Mrs.
Is	Female	Is	Single			Is	Ms.
Is	Male			<	8	Is	Young
						Is	?

Fig. 2-8

Let me run it again (just in case). Here we go:

```
RUN TEST: Test 3
Decision Run has been initialized
Decision DetermineCustomerGreeting: Define
Greeting Word
Greeting := Good Afternoon
Decision DetermineCustomerGreeting: Define
Salutation Word
Decision has been finalized
Validating results for the test <Test 3>
MISMATCH: variable 'Salutation' has value '?'
while 'Young' was expected
Test 3 was unsuccessful
1 test(s) out of 3 failed!
```

Fig.2-9

READER. Oops! What did happen? It says:

```
MISMATCH: variable 'Salutation' has value '?'
while 'Young' was expected
```

But why?

AUTHOR. Look at your third customer. This is a 5 years old female. So, naturally your first 4 rules failed, and then the default rules assigned '?' to the variable "Salutation" – exactly as it was supposed to do.

READER. Aha! Let me change the gender to "Male" and run our decision model again. Finally I got it right:

Conclusion: **Salutation Is Young**

AUTHOR. As you can see, you cannot overestimate the importance of testing! Even small changes could lead to results which are quite different from what you expected. **Never assume that your modified decision model will produce the correct results – TEST IT!**

READER. Now I see how the addition of even one rule can cause serious trouble. I think this example gives me a better understanding of how the decision model actually works.

AUTHOR. Good. Let's move forward with another enhancement. So far, we used only text variables and integer numbers. In addition, you may use real variables by defining their type as "double" instead of "int" in the Datatype tables. However, now I want to show you **how to deal with dates**.

READER. That would be great. Our own decision models would then be able to apply different rules on different dates.

AUTHOR. Actually DMN allows you to directly compare dates and to make basic arithmetic operations on them. To enhance our model with dates, let's assume that we do not know the customer's age but rather his/her Date of Birth. So, we may replace the condition "Age" in decision table "DefineSalutation" (see Fig. 2-8) with a condition "Date of Birth".

Instead of making changes in this table directly, I will first create a copy of the table in the same worksheet using Excel's Copy/Paste. Then I will comment out the previous table by adding "//" in front of the keyword "//DecisionTable".

READER. Why do you do that?

AUTHOR. Sometimes you want to try different implementations of your business logic. Who knows, maybe later on you would like to get back to the previous table. In general, people use standard version control systems such as SVN or GIT for their rule repositories. However, commenting out some decision constructs in the same Excel files is also a useful practice.

So, our new decision table "DefineSalutation" will look as follows:

DecisionTable DefineSalutation							
Condition		Condition		Condition		Conclusion	
Gender		Marital Status		Date of Birth		Salutation	
Is	Male			<	1/1/2010	Is	Mr.
Is	Female	Is	Married			Is	Mrs.
Is	Female	Is	Single			Is	Ms.
Is	Male			>=	1/1/2010	Is	Little

Fig. 2-10

READER. I guess we need to add the new variable "Date of Birth" to the glossary. Let me make the changes myself.

AUTHOR. Yes, go ahead.

READER. Here is the modified glossary:

Glossary glossary		
Variable	**Business Concept**	**Attribute**
Gender	Customer	gender
Marital Status		maritalStatus
Date of Birth		dob
Age		age
Current Hour		currentHour
Greeting		greeting
Salutation		salutation

Fig. 2-11

Now, I will add the attribute "dob" to the Datatype table "Customer". What type should I use for this attribute?

AUTHOR. You may simply use the type "Date" which is a valid Java type but you do not really have to know about it.

READER. OK, here is the corrected table:

Datatype Customer	
String	gender
String	maritalStatus
Date	dob
int	age
int	currentHour
String	greeting
String	salutation

Fig. 2-12

And now I will add the column "Date of Birth" to the Data table "customers". I guess I still may keep the attribute "Age" in it.

AUTHOR. Correct, even if our new decision table doesn't use it.

READER. Here is the updated table "customers":

Data Customer customers						
gender	maritalStatus	currentHour	greeting	salutation	dob	age
Gender	Marital Status	Current Hour	Greeting	Salutation	Date of Birth	Age
Female	Married	20	?	?	1/15/1972	45
Male	Single	11	?	?	10/19/1917	20
Male	Single	15	?	?	5/15/2012	5

Fig. 2-13

And, now I believe I can double-click on "run.bat"... YES! The results are the same as when we used the variable "Age". I must say it was quite a natural way to handle dates.

AUTHOR. You also can use predefined functions (or Java methods) to automatically calculate Age based on the Date of Birth, but we will talk about that later. See you next time.

Dialog-Session 3: Integrating Tested Decision Models with IT

Discussed Topics:

- Collaborative Rules and Decision Management
- Business Concepts and Java Decision Objects
- Request-Response
- Concatenating Strings
- Invoking Decision Models from Java Applications
- OpenRules Decision API
- Use of Java Inside Decision Tables

Related OpenRules Project:

- DecisionHelloWithRequestResponse
- DecisionHelloWithJava

AUTHOR. The DMN standard and supporting tools (such as OpenRules) are oriented mainly to business analysts or subject matter experts who are usually not software developers. While business people create and test their decision models, at some point of time they still want to transfer already tested models to their IT department to be integrated with actual business applications. During this session I will explain you how such integration can be achieved.

READER. Yes, even if I already understand how create my own datatypes and test cases, I know that in our production environment real data is coming from a database and the produced results should be saved back to the database. However, I really have no idea how our IT organized the database.

AUTHOR. That's exactly why we need to address the IT integration problems ASAP to make sure that decision model development does not become just a theoretical exercise. You, as a subject matter expert, will continue to stay in charge of the business logic by doing decision model maintenance and testing. However, we need to involve your IT for the integration. So, I suggest the following plan for today:

1) First we will slightly modify our decision model "Determine Customer Greeting" to make it look more like a real-world decision service;
2) Second, we will invite a software developer from your IT (let's call this person "DEVELOPER") to join this session and discuss with us all integration issues using the already tested decision model "Determine Customer Greeting".

READER. Sounds as a good plan. Let me make a quick call, so the DEVELOPER will join us remotely over the web.

AUTHOR. Please do it. During our webinar with the DEVELOPER, we may use Google Docs instead of local Excel. It will be an example of so-called "Collaborative Rules and Decision Management" – see the corresponding schema at this OpenRules web page.

OK, let's start with the first part. In the real-world, application decision models are usually used as services with clearly specified Requests (for input) and Responses (for output) objects. Probably your DEVELOPER expects to see such objects first and is less interested in your business logic. So, let's add Request and Response objects to our decision model "Determine Customer Greeting".

READER. You keep saying "objects" while so far I only remember one object "Customer" to whom you referred as a "Business Concept".

AUTHOR. You are right – we defined the business concept "Customer" in our Glossary, then specified a corresponding Datatype "Customer", and then defined specific test-customers in the Data table "customers".

READER. Probably real customers may be quite different from our definition of the Customer and contain much more information.

AUTHOR. Yes, but this is a good thing that we really did not worry how objects of the type "Customer" are actually represented in a database or how are they defined in a Java application that will use our decision model. In a way, our business concept "Customer" may be considered as our (decision model's) view of the actual object "Customer".

Now, I want to split out business concept "Customer" into 3 business concepts by modifying our Glossary in the following way:

Glossary glossary		
Variable	**Business Concept**	**Attribute**
Name	Customer	name
Gender		gender
Marital Status		maritalStatus
Current Hour	Request	currentHour
Location		location
Greeting	Response	greeting
Salutation		salutation
Result		result

Fig. 3-1

Dialog-Session 3

READER. I can see that you moved "Current Hour" to the new business concept "Request" and decision variables "Greeting and "Salutation" to another business concept "Response".

AUTHOR. Here is my reasoning for doing that. The "Current Hour" doesn't really belongs to the concept "Customer" as we may receive phone calls from the same customer during different hours of the day. Greeting and Salutation are also specific for a particular request, and I placed them in the separate concept "Response" that contains only output data.

READER. What about new variables "Location" and "Result"?

AUTHOR. We may use "Location" i.e. from where the phone call was received to define the Current Hour at this location. And I added "Result" to demonstrate how we can combine the generated Greeting, Salutation and customer's Name together.

READER. OK. Should not we modify our Data.xls file now?

AUTHOR. Yes, please do it yourself.

READER. No problem. Here are my new Datatype tables:

Datatype Customer	
String	name
String	maritalStatus
String	gender

Datatype Request	
String	location
int	currentHour

Datatype Response	
String	greeting
String	salutation
String	result

Fig. 3-2

And below are the properly modified Data tables:

Data Customer customers		
name	gender	maritalStatus
Customer Name	**Gender**	**Marital Status**
Robinson	Female	Married
Smith	Male	Single
Brown	Female	Single

Data Request requests
currentHour
Current Hour
20
11
14

Data Response responses		
greeting	salutation	result
Greeting	**Salutation**	**Result**
?	?	?
?	?	?
?	?	?

Fig. 3-3

AUTHOR. You didn't specify any location in the table "requests" but that is fine as we will not use this attributes in our model at this time. How about the table "testCases"?

READER. I am not sure how to modify it. We used to have only one column of the type "ActionUseObject" for the object "Customer"...

AUTHOR. You just can add two additional columns of the same type but for the objects Request and Response.

READER. Yes, of course! Here it goes:

DecisionTableTest testCases					
#	ActionUseObject	ActionUseObject	ActionUseObject	ActionExpect	ActionExpect
Test ID	**Request**	**Customer**	**Response**	**Greeting**	**Salutation**
Test 1	:= requests[0]	:= customers[0]	:= responses[0]	Good Evening	Mrs.
Test 2	:= requests[1]	:= customers[1]	:= responses[1]	Good Afternoon	Mr.
Test 3	:= requests[2]	:= customers[2]	:= responses[2]	Good Afternoon	Ms.

Fig. 3-4

Can I run this model now?

AUTHOR. Not yet. Remember we use a special table "decisionObjects" to map our business concept "Customer" to decision objects of the type "Customer? We need to modify this table as follows:

DecisionObject decisionObjects	
Business Concept	**Business Object**
Request	:= decision.get("Request")
Customer	:= decision.get("Customer")
Response	:= decision.get("Response")

Fig. 3-5

READER. OK. Now after running "run.bat" I received exactly the same results.

AUTHOR. Which is good as we didn't change anything in the business logic or test-customers. Now we are just better prepared for the integration with IT. We still have a few minutes before our web session with your DEVELOPER. Let's add one more table to fill out the output variable "Result".

READER. Let's do it. You said the Result should look like "Good Afternoon, Mrs. Robinson!".

AUTHOR. And here is a decision table "DefineResult" that has only one Action to define the variable "Result":

DecisionTable DefineResult
Action
Result
::= ${Greeting} + ", " + ${Salutation} + " " + ${Name} + "!"

Fig. 3-6

As you can see, here we use a special formula that concatenates 6 different strings:

- ${Greeting} – the generated Greeting
- ", " – a comma following by a space
- ${Salutation} – the generated Salutation
- " " – a space
- ${Name} – Customer's name
- "!" – the concluding exclamation sign.

In the actual DMN, you should be able to simply use a so-called FEEL expression that looks friendlier:

```
Greeting  + ", " + Salutation + " " + Name + "!"
```

However, the above formula demonstrates how the current OpenRules DMN implementation handles the concatenation of strings (as well as any other Java expression). It will be improved in future releases.

To make sure that this table will be executed by the decision model, we should add it to the table "Decision":

Decision DetermineCustomerGreeting	
Decisions	**Execute Decision Tables**
Define Greeting Word	DefineGreeting
Define Salutation Word	DefineSalutation
Define Result	DefineResult

Fig. 3-7

READER. When I tried to run this decision model, it additionally produced lines like:

```
Result: Good Afternoon, Ms. Brown!
```

AUTHOR. Very good. And now it's time to start our web-session with your DEVELOPER. Please upload our files Decision.xls, Glossary.xls and Data.xls to the Google's server to share them with the DEVELOPER using Google Docs. Don't worry, we will delete them from the server when we done.

DEVELOPER. Hello!

AUTHOR. Nice to meet you.

READER. Hi. As I told you ahead of time, we've completed our simple decision model called "Determine Customer Greeting".

So far we used Excel only to represent our business logic and created and ran different test cases. So, the model works and is being tested.

Now we want to integrate this model with a Java application. My ultimate objective is to make sure that you would be able to help me to similarly integrate our own decision models in the future.

DEVELOPER. What information does your model require as an input and what will it return as an output?

AUTHOR. This is the right question. As a developer, you may consider the decision model as a "black-box" that takes some input and produces some output.

READER. We've already defined all business concepts in the Excel file "Glossary.xls" – you can see it in the Google Docs now (Fig. 3-1).

AUTHOR. The glossary is actually a map between our business concepts Customer, Request, and Response and Java objects that should be provided by your Java application. The first column contains the business names of our decision variables, and the third column contains their technical counterparts. Preparing to this discussion, I've already opened our OpenRules's project "DecisionHelloWithJava" inside Eclipse IDE, and added 3 Java classes:

- Customer.java
- Request.java
- Response.java

They are basic Java beans and their attributes have exactly the same names as defined in the file Glossary.xls and the same types as defined in the file Data.xls – see the Datatype tables (Fig. 3-2).

DEVELOPER. OK, this is clear. I can see that you've already added all getters and setters to these Java classes.

AUTHOR. I simply used Eclipse Source +"Generate Getters and Setters..." to do it. Now I should show you a Java launcher that will create test-instances of these 3 classes and will pass then to our decision model using OpenRules Java API. Here is the proper code from the class Main.java:

```
public static void main(String[] args) {

    String fileName = "file:rules/main/Decision.xls";
    String decisionName = "DetermineCustomerGreeting";
    Decision decision = new Decision(decisionName,fileName);
    decision.put("FEEL", "On");
    decision.put("report", "On");

    Customer customer = new Customer();
    customer.setName("Robinson");
    customer.setGender("Female");
    customer.setMaritalStatus("Married");

    Request request = new Request();
    request.setCurrentHour(20);
    request.setLocation("NY");

    Response response = new Response();

    decision.put("Customer", customer);
    decision.put("Request", request);
    decision.put("Response", response);
    decision.execute();

    decision.log("\nDecision produced: " + response.getResult());
}
```

Fig. 3-8

AUTHOR. As you can see, first I created an instance of the OpenRules class Decision:

```
String fileName = "file:rules/main/Decision.xls";
```

```
String decisionName = "DetermineCustomerGreeting";
Decision decision =
                new  Decision(decisionName,fileName);
```

It refers to the main file “Decision.xls” located in the sub-folder “rules/main”. Look at this file in Google Docs. The “decisionName” corresponds to the name of the decision table on Fig. 3-7.

Then I created test-instances of the classes Customer, Request, and Response. The class Decision is a HashMap and you should put these 3 instances into the decision using names specified in the table “decisionObjects” of the file Decision.xls (Fig. 3-5). Now we are ready to execute the decision using the method

```
decision.execute();
```

You may print the produced result by displaying any Response’s attributes, e.g.:

```
decision.log(response.getResult());
```

DEVELOPER. So, let me summarize what you said. I am just creating an object of the class Decision, adding my input and output objects using the put-methods, and then calling Decision’s method execute(). It’s a very straightforward API!

AUTHOR. I am glad you like it. This API is well-documented in the User Manual, where you will find more specific features. Of course, you may get your data instances from a database, GUI, or other sources, convert them to Java objects, pass to the decision for processing, and save the decision’s results back to the original sources.

DEVELOPER. Do you provide any database interface?

AUTHOR. Yes, OpenRules comes with a simple JDBC interface, but you may use any 3rd party interface as well.

DEVELOPER. What if my application is not Java-based but rather .NET?

AUTHOR. No problem. You may deploy your OpenRules decision project as a web service and the proper WSDL interface for your .NET application will be automatically generated – read more here.

DEVELOPER. Can I try your application myself?

AUTHOR. I would recommend that you download the OpenRules Evaluation Version and open your own Eclipse with the provided workspace "openrules.dmn". Then you will be able to run and debug the discussed decision model from the project "DecisionHelloWithJava" using Eclipse Run/Debug As Java Application. You will also find many more complex decision models in this workspace.

READER. It seems you feel comfortable supporting my decision modeling efforts, don't you?

DEVELOPER. I think so. Anything else should I know?

AUTHOR. That's enough to integrate and run decision models. Also please make sure that your business people (decision modelers) utilize your standard version control system for maintenance of their Excel-based rule repositories.

DEVELOPER. Of course, I understand that we should keep all versions of their Excel files in-tact along with versions of our software that utilize these decision models.

AUTHOR. And finally, before you go, I want to share a few general thoughts. A good decision modeling practice frequently deals with what we, technical people, call "separation of concerns" or **correct distribution of knowledge between decision model and the code**. The DMN standard (and its OpenRules implementation) allows decision modelers to put a lot of formulas and even Java code directly into Excel. For example, the READER and I have already discussed how to add a customer's Date of Birth and Age to our model. With OpenRules, we can define a formula that calculates the current customer's Age based on the date of birth. For example, consider the following decision table:

DecisionTable DefineAge
Action
Age
::= Dates.yearsToday($D{Date of Birth})

Fig. 3-9

As you may guess, this decision table directly calls the static Java method "yearsToday" of the class Dates and passes to it the value of real (double) variable specified by the macro $D{Date of Birth}. The result will be assigned to the variable "Age".

DEVELOPER. I guess OpenRules uses "::=" as an indicator of Java expression.

AUTHOR. Yes, use "::=" in action-columns and ":=" in condition–columns.

DEVELOPER. Can they use my own Java methods or 3rd party Java libraries directly in Excel?

AUTHOR. Yes. To do that you should make sure that your jar-files are in the project's classpath and simply add a statement "import.java" to the standard Excel table "Environment" as in this example:

Environment	
include	../include/Rules.xls
	../include/Data.xls
	../include/Glossary.xls
	../../../openrules.config/DecisionTemplates.xls
import.java	com.openrules.tools.Dates

Fig. 3-10

DEVELOPER. Got it.

READER. Why didn't you tell me about these capabilities? Are they too technical for me?

AUTHOR. Not only for that reason. The knowledge of how to calculate a person's age based on his/her date of birth is not really business knowledge and does not belong to your business (!) decision model. Your developers can (and should!) guarantee that the object Customer already comes with the attributes Date of Birth and Age being synchronized. That's why the best decision models I've seen in my multi-year consulting practice were created by companies in which business specialists and software developers work in concert. These considerations complete our session today. Thank you to both of you and good luck developing and integrating good decision models together!

Suggested Exercises.

Consider a more complex decision model when various customer attributes including gender and marital status are missing or unknown – see e.g. this DMCommunity's Challenge "Greeting a Customer with Unknown Data".

Dialog-Session 4: Implementing Decision Model "Patient Therapy" with Complex Formulas

Discussed Topics:

Related OpenRules Project:

DecisionPatientTherapy

AUTHOR. You asked me to select a relatively simple but real use case from OpenRules decision modeling practice. Today I want us to implement a decision model for a problem that was offered to different business rules vendors by a large US hospital. The hospital planned to build an enterprise-level decisioning system that was supposed to help doctors determine patient therapies for different diagnoses. They used this problem as a prototype to compare the competitive capabilities of different products.

READER. Sounds interesting but keep in mind that my medical knowledge is very limited.

AUTHOR. Don't worry: my doctoral degree is in computer science and I hardly know more than you in the medical domain. However, the hospital asked us to concentrate on a very simplified scenario. Let's assume that a patient visited a doctor who determined that the patient has Acute Sinusitis. They asked us to implement the medication and dosing rules which are presented on Fig. 4-1 exactly as we received them from the hospital.

Medication Rules:

If Patient is 18 years old or older, then a therapy choice is Amoxicillin.
If Patient is younger than 18, a therapy choice is Cefuroxime.
If patient Penicillin allergic, therapy of choice is Levofloxacin.
Check if patient on active medication. Coumadin and Levofloxacin can result in reduced effectiveness of Coumadin. Produce the proper warning.

Dosing Rules:
For patients between 15 and 60, the dose is 500mg every 24 hours for 14 days.
If Patient's creatinine level > 1.4, commence creatinine clearance (CCr) calculation according to the formula:

$$\text{CCr, in mL/min} = \frac{(140 - \text{age}) \times \text{lean body weight [kg]}}{\text{PCr [mg/dL]} \times 72}$$

If patient's creatinine clearance < 50 ml/min, then the dose is 250mg every 24 hours for 14 days.
Dosing also depends on renal function, immune state, or liver function but the proper rules will be added later.

Fig. 4-1

What is your first impression about this problem?

READER. The medication rules do not look any more difficult than our greeting rules from the decision model "Determine Customer Greeting" we implemented in our previous sessions. However, their dosing rules include a very complicated formula to calculate "something" called Creatinine Clearance (CCr).

AUTHOR. It's good that we got an opportunity to learn how to implement complex formulas in DMN. But, I wouldn't worry about this now. As we already know, we should start with an answer to the question: what should our future decision model determine?

READER. I believe it should determine correct medications and their doses for different patients diagnosed with Acute Sinusitis.

AUTHOR. Good. Can you create a top-level DRD for this decision model?

READER. Do you mean Decision Requirement Diagram similar to our DRD for the decision model "DetermineCustomerGreeting"?

AUTHOR. Yes. Let's create a new folder with the name "DecisionPatientTherapy", and copy the old file "Decision.xls" with the DRD into its subfolder "rules". It's always better to reuse some previous work.

READER. No problem. Here is my first DRD for the new decision model which I called "DeterminePatientTherapy":

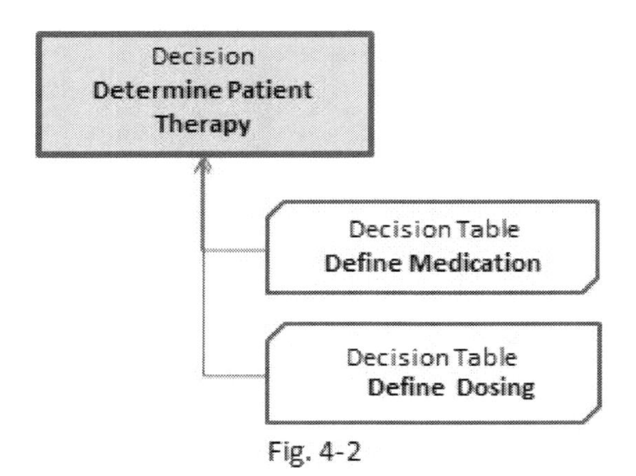

Fig. 4-2

I removed related business concepts (data) as we haven't discussed them yet.

AUTHOR. That's a good starting point. So, which business concepts will we use to implement business logic specified by the medication and dosing rules on Fig. 4-1?

READER. Similar to Customer in the previous model, we can define the business concept "Patient" for whom we need to know age, allergies, probably weight and more.

AUTHOR. Very good. We will also need a placeholder (a business concept) that will contain the diagnosis and the decision model output such as recommended medication and its dose. As this information belongs to a particular visit, I'd call this business concept "DoctorVisit".

READER. I've added these concepts to our DRD:

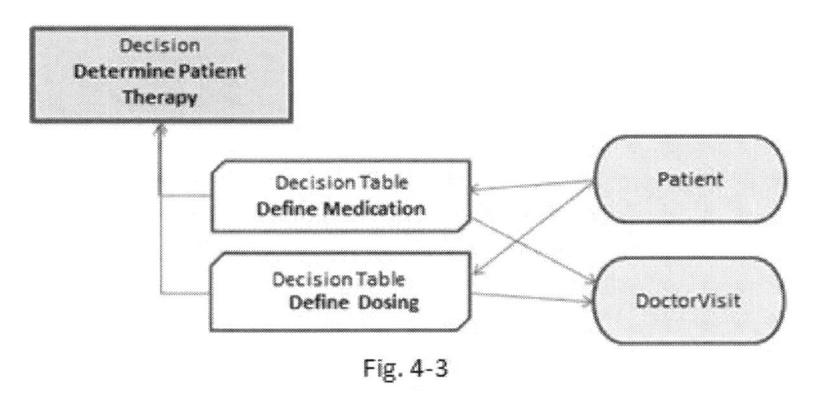

Fig. 4-3

AUTHOR. Can you explain your connecting arrows?

READER. Both rules "DefineMedication" and "DefineDosing" will use Patient's data, so the arrows are directed from Patient to these decision tables. And obviously, both table should save their results to the DoctorVisit.

AUTHOR. That's good for now. Can you create the proper table that will implement this diagram?

READER. It is very similar to what we did previously. Here it goes:

Decision DeterminePatientTherapy	
Decisions	**Execute Decision Tables**
Define Medication	DefineMedication
Define Dosing	DefineDosing

Fig. 4-4

AUTHOR. Good. We've already specified a high-level structure of our future decision model and given names to its key components. Now it's time to look at the actual decision logic described in the rules on Fig. 4-1. Let's start with the medication rules.

READER. The first 3 medication rules are:

1) If Patient is 18 years old or older, then the therapy choice is Amoxicillin
2) If Patient is younger than 18, then the therapy choice is Cefuroxime.
3) If Patient is allergic to Penicillin, then the therapy choice is Levofloxacin.

These rules look similar to our previous rules "DefineSalutation" in Fig. 2-1. But instead of "Salutation" they define a Recommended Medication (the therapy choice) based on a patient's age and possible allergies.

AUTHOR. Yes, you can use that table as a prototype for your new decision table "DefineMedication". Start with first two rules, and then we will talk about allergies.

READER. This is simple. Here is my decision table:

DecisionTable DefineMedication			
Condition		Conclusion	
Patient Age		Recommended Medication	
>=	18	Is	Amoxicillin
<	18	Is	Cefuroxime

Fig. 4-5

I can add here a second condition to express "If Patient is allergic to Penicillin".

AUTHOR. Not so quick. Of course, you may create a new decision variable "Patient Is Allergic to Penicillin" and check if it is "YES" or "NO". However, do you want to create similar decision variables for any other allergic medication?

READER. Of course, no.

AUTHOR. We also should think how all allergic medications can be presented in our business concept "Patient". Probably we can get an array (a list) of all medications, to which a particular patient is allergic. This array may contain several medications or none. The good news is that DMN allows us to use arrays of decision variables by just giving each array a unique name. Then we may use standard operators such as "Include" and "Do not include" with this array. Let me add the proper condition to your decision table. Here it is:

DecisionTable DefineMedication					
Condition		Condition		Conclusion	
Patient Age		**Patient Allergies**		**Recommended Medication**	
>=	18	Do not include	Penicillin	Is	Amoxicillin
<	18	Do not include	Penicillin	Is	Cefuroxime
		Include	Penicillin	Is	Levofloxacin

Fig. 4-6

READER. Hmm... I understand why we need to add "Do not include Penicillin" in all previous rules, but I don't really like it. What if we change the order of the rules to those in Fig. 4-7?

DecisionTable DefineMedication					
Condition		Condition		Conclusion	
Patient Age		**Patient Allergies**		**Recommended Medication**	
		Include	Penicillin	Is	Levofloxacin
>=	18			Is	Amoxicillin
<	18			Is	Cefuroxime

Fig. 4-7

AUTHOR. No problem, it will work as well. The reason is that OpenRules considers single-hit tables being so called "first-hit" (the DMN term) meaning that the rules are evaluated in the top-down order. If all conditions of the currently evaluated rule are satisfied, then the rule's conclusions will be executed and all remaining rules will be ignored. Otherwise, the next rule will be evaluated. However, your decision table on Fig. 4-7 depends on the order of rules while my table on Fig. 4-6 does not! It means it can be more difficult to insert new rules in your table.

READER. But my table looks much simpler and easier to read.

AUTHOR. In reality it's hard to give a general recommendation about which approach is better – it depends on concrete business conditions, such as how many changes do you expect in your decision table. We still may consider completely different approaches, e.g. splitting this table in two separate tables or to use a multi-hit table instead of our single-hit tables. We will get back to this problem later on. Now, please choose one of the tables, comment out the other one, and let's move on to dosing rules.

READER. But we also need to add another rule to our table. It states that if a patient is taking Coumadin that may interact with Levofloxacin.

AUTHOR. I'd suggest worrying about drug interaction rules later on, probably by creating another decision table. In general, we should never overcomplicate decision tables: it is better to create two different simple decision tables than to have a complex and difficult to understand single decision table. Let's first complete dosing rules, so we can test our, already complex enough, decision model ASAP.

READER. OK. The dosing rules themselves look like they can be presented using a decision table with three conditions for the patient's age, creatinine level, and creatinine clearance, plus one conclusion that will define the dosing. I think that is easy enough to do. What really concerns me is the complicated formula that specifies the patient's creatinine clearance as

$$\text{CCr, in mL/min} = \frac{(140 - \text{age}) \times \text{lean body weight [kg]}}{\text{PCr [mg/dL]} \times 72}$$

AUTHOR. Fortunately, what looks complex is frequently the simplest thing to do. The DMN standard and its OpenRules implementation allow you to write very complex formulas in a very intuitive way using the DMN FEEL language. Let me show how to do it the first time and then you will judge if it is complex or "friendly enough". Here is my decision table to calculate the patient's creatinine clearance:

DecisionTable CalculateCreatinineClearance
Action
Patient Creatinine Clearance
(140 - Patient Age) * Patient Weight / (Patient Creatinine Level * 72)

Fig. 4-8

READER. Wow! It looks exactly as in the specification on Fig. 4-1. You just use the decision variables "Patient Weight" for "lean body weight [kg]" and "Patient Creatinine Level" for "PCr[mg/dL], correct?

AUTHOR. That's exactly correct! We will assume that these values are attributes of our business concept "Patient". Please note that DMN FEEL allows me to freely use spaces and even apostrophes inside the variable names.

READER. Why do we still need to use a decision table to define a formula?

AUTHOR. Allow me to show you an alternative representation:

DecisionTableAssign CalculateCreatinineClearance	
Variable	Value
Patient Creatinine Clearance	(140 - Patient Age) * Patient Weight / (Patient Creatinine Level * 72)

Fig. 4-9

As you can see, this decision table has a new type defined by the keyword "DecisionTableAssign". This kind of table is used when you want to make multiple assignments using DMN FEEL formulas or OpenRules snippets. However, in our case, the standard decision table in Fig. 4-8 is a better choice, because if later on we decide to add conditions dealing with liver function, immune state, etc., a regular decision table will work much better than simple assignments.

READER. Now I can add a decision table "DefineDosing" by copying/pasting the table "DefineMedication". We already have a condition for "Patient Age". Wait a minute! How could I tell that a Patient Age is between 15 and 60? Should I add another column and use two different operators for "less" and "more"?

AUTHOR. You certainly could do that, but it would be more compact just to use the operator "Within" with a value cell specified as the interval "15..60". By default, the bounds 15 and 60 are included but you always can define your interval explicitly like "[15..60]" as required by DMN.

READER. No problems. Now I will replace condition "Patient Allergies" with "Patient's Creatinine Level" (as you called it in the formula above). Then I will add another condition for "Patient Creatinine Clearance" and replace the conclusion "Recommended Medication" with "Recommended Dose". My new decision table "DefineDosing" is presented in Fig. 4-10.

DecisionTable DefineDosing							
Condition		Condition		Condition		Conclusion	
Patient Age		Patient Creatinine Level		Patient Creatinine Clearance		Recommended Dose	
Within	15..60					Is	500mg every 24 hours for 14 days
		>	1.4	<	50	Is	250mg every 24 hours for 14 days

Fig. 4-10

AUTHOR. Apparently, you have become proficient at using decision tables. Your table looks good and it is almost identical to our plain English description.

READER. I like decision tables – they are really intuitive!

AUTHOR. You are right – we frequently understand our rules better when we are really trying to represent them in a decision table format. However, I have some questions. What if a patient is older than 60 and has a Creatinine Level less than 1.4 or Creatinine Clearance larger than 50?

READER. Do you mean that I have to add rules that cover all possible combinations of Patient Age, Creatinine Level, and Creatinine Clearance?

AUTHOR. The DMN's answer would be "Yes", your decision tables should be "complete" covering all possible situations. However, it is really difficult to satisfy this requirement when you have many conditions. The practical approach is to at least add one more rule for all "otherwise" situations.

READER. I got it. Here is the corrected table:

DecisionTable DefineDosing							
Condition		Condition		Condition		Conclusion	
Patient Age		Patient Creatinine Level		Patient Creatinine Clearance		Recommended Dose	
Within	[15..60]					Is	500mg every 24 hours for 14 days
		>	1.4	<	50	Is	250mg every 24 hours for 14 days
						Is	Not defined yet

Fig. 4-11

AUTHOR. Now we have the major decision logic implemented and you just need to follow the generic implementation steps to complete and test our decision model.

READER. OK. First, I will add a glossary and then test cases. My glossary will cover two business concepts:

- Patient
- Doctor Visit

Patient has Age, Allergies, Creatinine Level and Clearance, i.e. those variables that we used in the decision tables and that can be attributed to a patient. All other variables like Recommended Medication and Dose are defined during a visit should belong to the concept "DoctorVisit". Here is my version of the glossary:

Glossary glossary		
Decision Variable	**Business Concept**	**Attribute**
Recommended Medication	DoctorVisit	recommendedMedication
Recommended Dose		recommendedDose
Patient Age	Patient	age
Patient Weight		weight
Patient Allergies		allergies
Patient Creatinine Level		creatinineLevel
Patient Creatinine Clearance		creatinineClearance

Fig. 4-12

AUTHOR. So far so good. Let's proceed to test cases.

READER. First, I will create Datatype and Data tables that correspond to our business concepts. Here they are:

Datatype Patient	
String	name
int	age
double	creatinineLevel
double	creatinineClearance
String	allergies
double	weight

Datatype DoctorVisit	
String	recommendedMedication
String	recommendedDose

Fig. 4-13

I copied/pasted the attributes used in the Glossary above. I also added "name" to identify different test cases.

AUTHOR. Good. But now I need to show you how to deal with arrays. The attribute "allergies" is an array of strings and should have type "String[]" instead of "String" like below:

Datatype Patient	
String	name
int	age
double	creatinineLevel
double	creatinineClearance
String[]	allergies
double	weight

Fig. 4-14

READER. I got it – two characters [] after type "String" specify an array. Can I also write int[]?

AUTHOR. Yes, you can. Now you can start preparing your Patient Data table.

READER. Here we go:

Data Patient patients					
name	age	allergies	creatinineLevel	creatinineClearance	weight
Name	**Age**	**Allergies**	**Creatinine Level**	**Creatinine Clearance**	**Weight**
John Smith	58	Penicillin	2.00	44.42	78
Mary Smith	65		1.80	48.03	83

Fig. 4-15

AUTHOR. Good. What if John Smith has multiple allergies, e.g. Penicillin and Streptomycin? In this case, you may split your cell, in which you placed "Penicillin", into two (or more) horizontal sub-rows. See how I did it in Fig. 4-16:

Data Patient patients					
name	age	allergies	creatinineLevel	creatinineClearance	weight
Name	**Age**	**Allergies**	**Creatinine Level**	**Creatinine Clearance**	**Weight**
John Smith	58	Penicillin	2.00	44.42	78
		Streptomycin			
Mary Smith	65		1.80	48.03	83

Fig. 4-16

READER. It is really nice.

AUTHOR. And it is so natural to do these kinds of changes in Excel or Google Docs. Now please add test cases for DoctorVisit.

READER. Here they are:

Data DoctorVisit visits	
recommendedMedication	recommendedDose
Recommended Medication	**Recommended Dose**
?	?
?	?

Fig. 4-17

Now I believe I can also define the table "testCases" for these two visits.

AUTHOR. Put only "Recommended Medication" in the expected results and make your best guess.

READER. Here we go:

DecisionTableTest testCases			
#	ActionUseObject	ActionUseObject	ActionExpect
Test ID	DoctorVisit	Patient	Recommended Medication
Test 1	:= visits[0]	:= patients[0]	Levofloxacin
Test 2	:= visits[1]	:= patients[1]	Amoxicillin

Fig. 4-18

AUTHOR. We should run our decision model to see if your expected results are correct. Do we have everything in place?

READER. Let me check. Our main table "Decision" was defined in Fig. 4-3, but apparently it was missing the call for our Creatinine Clearance formula. I've added it now:

Decision DeterminePatientTherapy	
Decisions	Execute Decision Tables
Define Medication	DefineMedication
Define Creatinine Clearance	CalculateCreatinineClearance
Define Dosing	DefineDosing

Fig. 4-19

AUTHOR. And finally, let's update the configuration file "define.bat":

```
set FILE_NAME=rules/DecisionPatientTherapy.xls
set DECISION_NAME=DeterminePatientTherapy
```

Please double-click on "run.bat" and let's see our first execution results.

READER. They are presented in Fig. 4-20.

```
RUN TEST: Test 1
Decision Run has been initialized
Decision DeterminePatientTherapy: Define Medication
Conclusion: Recommended Medication Is Levofloxacin
[Levofloxacin]
Decision DeterminePatientTherapy: Define Creatinine
Clearance
Assign: Patient Creatinine Clearance = (140 -
Patient Age) * Patient Weight / (Patient Creatinine
Level * 72) [44.416666666666664]
Decision DeterminePatientTherapy: Define Dosing
Conclusion: Recommended Dose Is 500mg every 24
hours for 14 days [500mg every 24 hours for 14
days]
Decision has been finalized
Validating results for the test <Test 1>
Test 1 was successful

RUN TEST: Test 2
Decision Run has been initialized
Decision DeterminePatientTherapy: Define Medication
Conclusion: Recommended Medication Is Amoxicillin
[Amoxicillin]
Decision DeterminePatientTherapy: Define Creatinine
Clearance
Assign: Patient Creatinine Clearance = (140 -
Patient Age) * Patient Weight / (Patient Creatinine
Level * 72) [48.032407407407]
Decision DeterminePatientTherapy: Define Dosing
Conclusion: Recommended Dose Is 250mg every 24
hours for 14 days [250mg every 24 hours for 14
days]
Decision has been finalized
Validating results for the test <Test 2>
Test 2 was successful
All 2 tests succeeded!
```

Fig. 4-20

Both tests produced the expected results! Could you please explain these results of our creatinine clearance calculation?

```
Assign: Patient Creatinine Clearance = (140 -
Patient Age) * Patient Weight / (Patient's
Creatinine Level * 72) [44.416666666666664]
```

AUTHOR. The execution protocol shows the formula itself and then the result in brackets.

READER. Why is it 44.416666666666664? Can we limit it to only two digits after the decimal dot?

AUTHOR. You can do it by switching from DMN FEEL to the OpenRules snippet shown in Fig.4-21:

DecisionTable CalculateCreatinineClearance
Action
Patient Creatinine Clearance
:= format((140 - $I{Patient Age}) * $R{Patient Weight} / ($R{Patient Creatinine Level} * 72))

Fig. 4-21

READER. Now it produces

```
Assign: Patient Creatinine Clearance = 44.42
```

AUTHOR. You may use Java snippets every time you need to invoke standard or 3rd party Java functions. That's enough about formulas.

Now it's time to add the required drug interaction rules.

READER. They were formulated as

> Check if patient on active medication. Coumadin and Levofloxacin can result in reduced effectiveness of Coumadin. Produce the proper warning.

think we just need to add one more variable "Patient Active Medication" and check if it is Coumadin or not.

AUTHOR. I recommend placing this logic in a separate decision table "WarnAboutDrugInteraction" as this logic potentially may become much more complex. We will use a special action-column of the type "Message" to produce a warning about drug conflicts as in Fig. 4-22:

DecisionTable WarnAboutDrugInteraction				
Condition		Condition		Message
Recommended Medication		Patient Active Medication		Warning
Is	Levofloxacin	Is	Coumadin	Coumadin and Levofloxacin can result in reduced effectiveness of Coumadin.

Fig. 4-22

READER. But we cannot run the modified model until we add the new variable "Patient Active Medication" to the glossary, and our datatype and data tables. Here are the proper changes:

Glossary glossary		
Decision Variable	Business Concept	Attribute
Recommended Medication	DoctorVisit	recommendedMedication
Recommended Dose		recommendedDose
Patient Age	Patient	age
Patient Weight		weight
Patient Allergies		allergies
Patient Creatinine Level		creatinineLevel
Patient Creatinine Clearance		creatinineClearance
Patient Active Medication		activeMedication

Fig. 4-23

Datatype Patient	
String	name
int	age
double	creatinineLevel
double	creatinineClearance
String[]	allergies
double	weight
String	activeMedication

Fig. 4-24

Data Patient patients						
name	age	allergies	creatinineLevel	creatinineClearance	weight	activeMedication
Name	**Age**	**Allergies**	**Creatinine Level**	**Creatinine Clearance**	**Weight**	**Active Medication**
John Smith	58	Penicillin	2.00	44.42	78	Coumadin
		Streptomycin				
Mary Smith	65		1.80	48.03	83	

Fig. 4-25

AUTHOR. Don't forget to add "WarnAboutDrugInteraction" to our main table "Decision".

READER. Of course, here it is:

Decision DeterminePatientTherapy	
Decisions	**Execute Decision Tables**
Define Medication	DefineMedication
Define Creatinine Clearance	CalculateCreatinineClearance
Define Dosing	DefineDosing
Check Drug Interaction	WarnAboutDrugInteraction

Fig. 4-26

AUTHOR. Let's run it and look at the results.

READER. The execution results are the same except now as we expected Test 1 produced this warning:

```
Decision DeterminePatientTherapy: Check Drug
Interaction
Coumadin and Levofloxacin can result in reduced
effectiveness of Coumadin. [produced by
WarnAboutDrugInteraction]
```

Fig. 4-27

AUTHOR. Very good! This completes our 4th dialog-session. Hope it was productive.

READER. Very productive, thank you! Only one more question. Will you show me another representation of our table "DefineMedication" for which we created two alternative single-hit decision tables?

AUTHOR. We will do it at the beginning of the next dialog-session when we learn about multi-hit decision tables. See you next time.

Suggested Exercises.

1. Add more test cases that deal with the problem of incompleteness in our decision tables and analyze the received results.
2. Add a check for the encounter diagnosis "Acute Sinusitis" to the already created decision model.

Dialog-Session 5: Single-Hit and Multi-Hit Decision Tables

Discussed Topics:

Related OpenRules Project:

DecisionVacationDays
DecisionUpSell
DecisionLoanPreQualification

AUTHOR. Today we will learn more about different types of decision tables, discuss their execution logic, and when and how better to use them. Decision tables, in general, are known and have been widely used for more than 40 years [8]. The DMN standard specifies two major types of decision tables:

- Single-Hit Decision Tables
- Multi-Hit (or Multiple-Hit) Decision Tables

So far, we have considered only single-hit decision tables which finish their work as soon as at least one rule is executed (its conditions are satisfied) or they reach their end without satisfying any rule. Such decision table may hit no more than one rule – that's why we call them "**single-hit**". By the way, along with the keyword "DecisionTable" at the left top corner you can use its synonym "**DecisionTableSingleHit**".

READER. During the last session we created two different representations of the decision table "DefineMedication" in Figures 4-6 and 4-7. I understand that both of them are examples of single-hit decision tables. I still like my table on Fig. 4-7, you promised to show an alternative representation.

AUTHOR. Yes, and to do this I want to use a multi-hit decision table. I will use my table in Fig.4-6 as a prototype and will make only two changes:

1) Replace the keyword "DecisionTable" with "**DecisionTableMultiHit**"
2) Remove values for Patient Allergies from the first two rules.

Here is our first example of a multi-hit decision table:

DecisionTableMultiHit DefineMedication					
Condition		Condition		Conclusion	
Patient Age		Patient Allergies		Recommended	
>=	18			Is	Amoxicillin
<	18			Is	Cefuroxime
		Include	Penicillin	Is	Levofloxacin

Fig. 5-1

READER. Wow! Now it looks almost like my table in Fig. 4-7: the only difference is that your third rule was the first one in my table.

AUTHOR. Not only the rules order is important in both cases (4-7 and 5-1). The decision table type "DecisionTableMultiHit" assumes a different behavior:

1) First (before executing any rules) a multi-hit decision table evaluates all rules and marks those whose conditions are satisfied as "to be executed"
2) Then it tries to execute ALL "to be executed" rules in the natural top-down order.

Thus, a multi-hit decision table may execute multiple rules, for which all conditions are satisfied - that's why we call such table "**multi-hit**".

READER. I actually like it. I think the third rule in the table 5-1 may override the results of a previously executed rule.

AUTHOR. Try to execute it and we will look at the results.

READER. The final results are the same. However, for the first test when our 58 years old patient is allergic to Penicillin, we received not one but two(!) conclusions:

```
Decision DeterminePatientTherapy: Define
Medication
Conclusion: Recommended Medication Is Amoxicillin
[Amoxicillin]
Conclusion: Recommended Medication Is Levofloxacin
[Levofloxacin]
```

Fig. 5-2

It means that our first rule recommended Amoxicillin. The second rules was omitted as our patient is older than 18. And finally our third rule that does not care about Age, decided to replace the recommended medication with Levofloxacin!

AUTHOR. That's exactly what we wanted and is very similar to the initial specification in plain English.

READER. I think it is the best representation so far!

AUTHOR. I don't want you to be overly-optimistic. There are no "golden" rule for which type of decision table is the best – it really depends on your particular case: how many rules this table has, how it's going to be modified in the future, etc. It would be much more productive if you are aware of different available options and gain experience applying them in various situations. So, let's consider more examples.

READER. I love to learn by example.

AUTHOR. One of the most notorious example was presented as a Challenge in December of 2015 by Decision Management Community (http://DMCommunity.org). It's called "Vacation Days" and there are more than 19 different solutions submitted for this Challenge. Later on you may compare all of them along with an analysis provided by Prof. Jan Vanthienen. Here is the problem definition:

The number of vacation days depends on age and years of service.

Every employee receives at least 22 days.
Additional days are provided according to the following criteria:

1) Only employees younger than 18 or at least 60 years, or employees with at least 30 years of service will receive 5 extra days.

2) Employees with at least 30 years of service and also employees of age 60 or more, receive 3 extra days, on top of possible additional days already given.

3) If an employee has at least 15 but less than 30 years of service, 2 extra days are given. These 2 days are also provided for employees of age 45 or more. These 2 extra days can not be combined with the 5 extra days.

Fig. 5-3

I want us to implement these rules using a single-hit or a multi-hit decision table.

READER. OK, let's call our decision table "DefineVacationDays". I will start with a single-hit decision table similar to our previous "DefineMedication" table. Instead of "Recommended Medication" it should define the variable "Vacation Days" depending on variables "Age" and "Service". I believe we just need to list different combinations of Age and Service and then I can use different formulas to define the Vacation Days.

AUTHOR. I can see that you are a quick learner. Just to be more precise, I'd call your conditions "Age in Years" and "Years in Service" – it will also keep us closer to the specification.

READER. Here is my version using a singly-hit decision table:

DecisionTable DefineVacationDays		
If	If	Then
Age in Years	**Years of Service**	**Vacation Days**
<18		22 + 5
[18..45)	<15	22
[18..45)	[15..30)	22 + 2
[18..45)	>=30	22 + 5 + 3
[45..60)	<15	22 + 2
[45..60)	[15..30)	22 + 2
[45..60)	>=30	22 + 5 + 3
60+		22 + 5 +3

Fig. 5-4

AUTHOR. This is a very good solution! It really looks similar to what was described in plain English. I like your solution! And you freely used the DMN FEEL formulas without even thinking about it. Even if you change the table's type to

"DecisionTableMultiHit" the results will be the same because all conditions in your representation are **mutually-exclusive**!

READER. I even can change the rules order and it should continue to work. So, wouldn't you always recommend making all rules in a decision table mutually-exclusive? It could be our "golden" rule...

AUTHOR. Unfortunately, it's wishful thinking. In this particular case, for only two decision variables you created 8 different combinations (rules). Let's assume that the company decides to change its vacation policy and give different vacation days to people who worked for less than 5, 10, and 15 years.

READER. I will just need to add more rules adding new conditions in the second column...

AUTHOR. Now, think what will happen if we also need to consider additional factors, e.g. Work Type, Gender, etc. When the number of variables inside a decision table grows just a little bit (mathematicians call it logarithmically) the number of their possible combinations grows really fast (exponentially). Unfortunately, many real-world decision tables have hundreds or even thousands of rules and some of them depend on each other.

READER. Yep.. I believe I myself can give you a few examples of such large decision tables from my own business domain.

AUTHOR. Don't get me wrong: it is a very good practice to try to cover ALL possible combinations of decision variables by making your decision table **complete** with all rules being mutually-exclusive. Do it whenever you can!

More than that, experienced decision modelers recommend splitting large decision tables into multiple smaller tables, which may follow this "golden" rule - see for example the design pattern "Divide and Conquer" in [3]. Unfortunately, it is not always possible and we have to consider other methods to minimize the total number of rules in our decision tables.

Now I want to use the same problem to show you how to accumulate some values using multi-hit decision tables. In this problem, every employee receives at least 22 vacation days – note that you repeated this value inside every rule!

READER. It annoyed me too but...

AUTHOR. What if we give everybody 22 days unconditionally at the very beginning and then different rules will add extra days based on different situations?

READER. I like this idea – probably in this case I wouldn't need to consider all possible situations but only those described in the specification. But how can I add a value to the variable "Vacation Days"?

AUTHOR. Let me explain this feature using an example of the multi-hit table:

DecisionTableMultiHit ApplicantCreditScoreDecisionTable				
If	If	If	Conclusion	
Applicant Number of Default Payments in Last 12 Months	Applicant had declared Bankrupcy	Applicant Years with Current Account Bank	Applicant Credit Score	
			=	0
[1..3]			+=	100
[4..6]			+=	50
>6			+=	0
0			+=	250
	TRUE		+=	0
	FALSE		+=	250
		< 1	+=	50
		[1..3]	+=	150
		>3	+=	250

Fig. 5-5

As you can see, OpenRules provides a special assign-operator "+=" used in the conclusions. In this example, the first rule uses the operator "=" to assign 0 to the variable "Applicant Credit Score". The second and all other rules use the operator "+=" to increment Applicant Credit Score with the proper rule value. Along with the operator "+=" you may use "-=", "*=", and "/=". Actually, this is an OpenRules implementation of the "collect operators" defined by DMN.

READER. Great! Now I think I know how to implement the "DefineVacationDays" table in a new way. I will try to write the rules exactly as they are presented in the specification. Here we go:

DecisionTableMultiHit DefineVacationDays			
Condition	Condition	Conclusion	
Age in Years	Years of Service	Vacation Days	
		=	22
<18		+=	5
>=18	>=30	+=	5
>=60	<30	+=	5
	>=30	+=	3
>=60	<30	+=	3
[45..60)	<30	+=	2
<45	[15..30)	+=	2

Fig. 5-6

AUTHOR. Right, this multi-hit table should produce the same results as the single-hit table 5-4. Which table do you like more?

READER. We clearly defined 22 days as the minimum, but we didn't win in the total number of rules - both tables have 8 rules. However, it probably will be easier to add more service intervals or new factors you mentioned earlier.

AUTHOR. That's true: there are always pros and cons. It seems to me that your table 5-4 is still better organized; it covers the different intervals in a consistent fashion. It's not immediately clear if table 5-6 covers all intervals or if it leaves some gaps. Anyway, now you have more options to choose from. More than that, I can offer you another option that is based on the design pattern "Divide and Conquer" [3] which sometimes is also called "Separation of Concerns".

READER. Another type of the decision table?

AUTHOR. Not really. In our previous solutions we put all rules inside one decision table. However, our business logic on the very high-level gives each employee 22 vacation days as a base plus 2, 3 or 5 extra days to those who are eligible for them. Why not create intermediate decision variables "Eligible for 5 Extra Days", "Eligible for 3 Extra Days", and "Eligible for 2 Extra Days" and present our business logic as on Fig. 5-7?

DecisionTableMultiHit CalculateVacationDays				
If	If	If	Conclusion	
Eligible for Extra 5 Days	Eligible for Extra 3 Days	Eligible for Extra 2 Days	Vacation Days	
			=	22
TRUE			+=	5
	TRUE		+=	3
FALSE		TRUE	+=	2

Fig. 5-7

It will allow us to define the eligibility for extra days in a separate, very simple table instead of mixing everything together. For example, here is a decision table for 5 extra days eligibility:

DecisionTable SetEligibleForExtra5Days		
If	If	Then
Age in Years	Years of Service	Eligible for Extra 5 Days
< 18		TRUE
>= 60		TRUE
	>= 30	TRUE
		FALSE

Fig. 5-8

READER. Wow, that simplifies everything dramatically! Let me put together the table for 3 and 5 extra days. Here we go:

DecisionTable SetEligibleForExtra3Days		
If	If	Then
Age in Years	Years of Service	Eligible for Extra 3 Days
	>= 30	TRUE
>= 60		TRUE
		FALSE

DecisionTable SetEligibleForExtra2Days		
If	If	Then
Age in Years	Years of Service	Eligible for Extra 2 Days
	[15..30)	TRUE
>= 45		TRUE
		FALSE

Fig. 5-9

AUTHOR. Have you noticed that the main table in Fig. 5-7 is multi-hit while other 3 tables are single-hit?

READER. Yes, and I really like such a combined use of multi-hit and single-hit decision tables. Now the extra days eligibility rules are completely independent of each other, and we do not really care about the rule order inside the main decision table.

AUTHOR. That's true. In spite of the fact that the latest solution takes 4 decision tables instead of one, it is more clear and easy to maintain.

Now let's talk about the default values. Where did we put the default (or initial) values in multi-hit tables?

READER. In the multi-hit table in Figures 5-6 and 5-7 we put the default value 22 in the very first rule.

AUTHOR. Now we may formulate the common rule:

> *"If you use a **multi-hit** decision table, always put the default value in the very **first** unconditional rule"*

READER. And for single-hit decision tables such as in Fig. 5-9, we may formulate another common rule:

> *"If you use a **single-hit** decision table, always put the default value in the very **last** unconditional rule"*

AUTHOR. Correct. Just note that for complete decision tables such as your initial table in Fig. 5-4 you do not have to define any default values.

READER. I am really excited. Such a simple problem gave us an opportunity to consider so many different options!

AUTHOR. I am glad you appreciate the power of decision tables. Any questions at this point?

READER. Yes. When I tried to read the DMN specification, I remember I was confused by various hit policies abbreviated to one letter like "U", "F", "P", etc. So far, you didn't mention them at all. Will we use these hit policies?

AUTHOR. Well… You are right that the current version of DMN assigns special characters to 7 different hit policies which in reality specify different decision table execution algorithms. There are 4 hit policies for single-hit tables: **U**nique, **A**ny, **P**riority, **F**irst. There are 3 hit policies for multi-hit decision tables: **O**utput, **R**ule, **C**ollect – you may find their description in the DMN specification [1] on page 82. Some experts prefer the policy "U", others – "A", but the majority of experts recommend avoiding the policy "**P**". OpenRules considers only two major policies:

- single-hit
- multi-hit.

Our real-world experience shows that OpenRules can handle all listed types of hit policies (except "Priority") without asking a user to specify them explicitly. So, in this guide you only have to choose between single-hit and multi-hit decision tables assuming you understand their behavior as described above.

READER. It's OK with me to avoid unnecessary complexity. But in considering the decision table execution algorithms, to tell you the truth, I don't understand why is it important that a multi-hit table evaluates the rules before executing them? We could just say that a multi-hit decision table executes all satisfied rules in top-down order…

AUTHOR. Now it's my turn to say "Wow!" We really need to clarify the way in which multi-hit tables are being executed.

Let's consider a very simple example. Let's assume that you need to create a decision table that does the following:

```
If X is equal to 1 make it 2.
If X is equal to 2 make it 1.
```

READER. It is trivial. Here is the decision table:

DecisionTable Swap	
If	Then
X	X
1	2
2	1

Fig. 5-10

AUTHOR. Yes, for this single-hit table everything is clear: only the first **or** the second rule will be executed. But what if we make this table multi-hit as below?

DecisionTableMultiHit Swap	
If	Then
X	X
1	2
2	1

Fig. 5-11

READER. Let's say that initially X is equal to 1. Then the first rule will be executed and X will become 2. Then the second rule also should be executed as X is equal 2, and X will become 1 again. So, this multi-hit table will not work!

AUTHOR. You are wrong, and the reason is exactly the first point of the multi-hit table behavior. Let me repeat it again:

1) First (before executing any rules) a multi-hit decision table evaluates all rules and marks those whose conditions are satisfied as "to be executed"
2) Then it tries to execute ALL "to be executed" rules in the natural top-down order.

Thus, at the very beginning only the first rule will be evaluated as "to be executed", and independent of the first rule the second one will not be executed. And if X is equal to 2, then only the second rule will be first evaluated as "to be executed" and then it will be really executed by assigning the value 1 to X. So, both single-hit and multi-hit tables will produce the correct results!

READER. Now I do understand that evaluation before execution is really important. Does DMN clarifies this point as well?

AUTHOR. Unfortunately, it does not. Instead it simply prohibits using the same variables in both conditions and actions in order to avoid so called "side effects". At the same time DMN FEEL allows you to execute other decision tables and different functions from the decision table cells. It means they might indirectly change the values of variables used inside conditions of this decision table, and we might get "side effects" anyway. At OpenRules, we believe it is better not the limit a user's capabilities but rather make your execution engine powerful enough to prevent possible errors.

We still have time today, and I want to discuss one more important observation about decision tables. It is very important to stress that

> *"All conditions are connected by the logical AND"*
> *"All actions/conclusions in decision tables are connected by the logical AND"*

For example, when we read the 4th rule in the decision table in Fig. 5-6 we say:

"IF Age in Years >= 60 AND Years In Service < 30
THEN Increment Vacation Days by 5"

We do not use the logical OR, correct?

READER. Correct, but we actually define OR-conditions when we add additional rules to the same decision table.

AUTHOR. Yes, this is also an important common convention for decision tables.

READER. Still, what if I need to express the following condition "If Employment Status Is Unemployed or Retired Then do something"? Should I create separate rules for Unemployed, Retired, and possibly more values of the Employment Status?

AUTHOR. Of course, not! DMN allows a user to list the possible values like "Unemployed, Retired" by using comma inside the same cell. For example, Fig. 5-12 shows a fragment of an OpenRules decision table from the project "DecisionUpSell". As you can see, to decide whether a Customer profile is New, Bronze **or** Silver it uses the operator "Is One Of" with different values separated by a comma. Similarly, you may use operators "Include" and "Do Not Include".

DecisionTable DefineUpSellProducts					
Condition		Condition		Condition	
Customer Profile		Customer Products		Customer Products	
Is One Of	New,Bronze, Silver	Include	Checking Account	Do Not Include	Saving Account
Is One Of	New,Bronze, Silver	Include	Checking Account, Overdraft Protection	Do Not Include	CD with 25 basis point increase, Money Market Mutual Fund, Credit Card
Is One Of	New,Bronze, Silver	Include	Checking Account, Saving Account	Do Not Include	CD with 25 basis point increase, Money Market Mutual Fund, Credit Card
Is One Of	Gold	Include	Checking Account	Do Not Include	CD with 25 basis point increase, Money Market Mutual Fund, Web Banking

Fig. 5-12

READER. I see, the comma inside a list of values serves as an "OR". What if a value in the list already contains a comma?

AUTHOR. In this case, instead of a comma, you may specify another separator, e.g. "$". All you need to do is to add this separator at the end of you operator, e.g. "Is One Of separated by $".

Another complete example of similar "OR-expressions" is shown in Fig. 5-13. It is borrowed from the standard OpenRules project "DecisionLoanPreQualification". I recommend that you download, analyze, and do some experiments with these simple enough decision projects.

DecisionTableMultiHit DetermineDebtResearchResult								
If	If	If	If	If	Condition		If	Then
Mortgage Holder	Outside Credit Score	Loan Holder	Credit Card Balance	Education Loan Balance	Internal Credit Rating		Internal Analyst Opinion	Debt Research Result
Yes								High
No	(100..550)							High
No	(550..900]	Yes	<=0					Mid
No	(550..900]	Yes	>0	>0				High
No	(550..900]	Yes	>0	<=0	Is One Of	A, B, C		High
No	(550..900]	Yes	>0	<=0	Is One Of	D, F		Mid
No	(550..900]	No	>0					Low
No	(550..900]	No	<=0	<=0				Low
No	(550..900]	No	<=0	>0	Is One Of	D, F		High
No	(550..900]	No	<=0	>0	Is One Of	A, B, C		Low
							High	High
							Mid	Mid
							Low	Low

Fig. 5-13

READER. I will certainly look at these examples.

AUTHOR. Let's call it a day. See you next time.

Suggested Exercises.

1. Modify the decision model "DecisionVacationDays" by giving employees who served more than 20 years 4 extra days.
2. Analyze the decision model "DecisionUpSell". Modify it by adding an additional Customer Profile "Platinum" .
3. Analyze the decision model "Decision Loan Pre-Qualification". Modify it by changing the decision table "DetermineDebtResearchResults" to become single-hit instead of multi-hit, and explain why the results are different.

Dialog-Session 6: Scorecards, Accumulating Values, and Dealing with Collections of Objects

Discussed Topics:

Related OpenRules Project:

DecisionCreaditCardApplication
DecisionAggregatedValues

AUTHOR. Today we will begin with an analysis of a special type of decision table called a "scorecard". Some business decisions depend on a combination of many factors and it is difficult to name all possible values of a target decision variable. In such cases it may be better to define a numerical score that represents the weighted contributions of different factors. Usually, such a score is a numerical decision variable with an established range, e.g. FICO Score is defined between 300 and 850.

READER. I believe we plan to use scorecards in our own application as well.

AUTHOR. If you go back to previous session and look at the Fig. 5-5, it already provided you with an example of the scorecard. **"Scorecard" is a regular multi-hit decision table** that accumulates a numerical score in one decision variable based on various combinations of other decision variables.

READER. Will we look at a complete decision model that uses a scorecard?

AUTHOR. The scorecard in Fig. 5-5 was a fragment of a real decision table that calculates a credit score for a credit card applicant. The decision model "DecisionCreditCardApplication" was proposed by Nick Broom and is described at the DMCommunity website. I am certain you would not have a problem following this decision model yourself.

However, I want us to quickly walk through the business logic that determines if an applicant is eligible to receive a credit card. Here is the proper eligibility decision:

Decision ApplicantCreditCardEligibilityDecision	
Decisions	**Execute Decision Table**
Determine Applicant Credit Score	ApplicantCreditScoreDecisionTable
Determine Applicant Balance Transfer Credit Card Eligibility	ApplicantBalanceTransferCreditCardEligibilityDecisionTable
Determine Applicant Credit Card Eligibility	ApplicantCreditCardEligibilityDecisionTable

Fig. 6-1

READER. OK, I can see that first we need to define Applicant Credit Score and then execute two more sub-decisions.

AUTHOR. Here is a complete scoring decision table:

DecisionTableMultiHit ApplicantCreditScoreDecisionTable					
If	If	If	If	Conclusion	
Applicant Number of Default Payments in Last 12 Months	Applicant had declared Bankrupcy	Applicant Years with Current Account Bank	Applicant Amount of Available Credit Used Percentage	Applicant Credit Score	
				=	0
[1..3]				+=	100
[4..6]					50
>6					0
0					250
	TRUE				0
	FALSE				250
		< 1			50
		[1..3]			150
		>3			250
			[0..24]		200
			[25..49]		249
			[50..74]		150
			[75..100]		100
			>100		0

Fig. 6-2

What can you say about this table?

READER. First of all, it is a multi-hit decision (specified by the keyword "DecisionTableMultiHit" in the top-left corner). Applicant Credit Score is being accumulated based on different conditions defined by 4 independent attributes of the applicant. I also noticed that the author of the table decided to include rules that do not really change the score (by adding 0). Probably it's done for completeness – what if we later decide to change them?

AUTHOR. Very good. And the following table defines Balance Transfer Credit Card Eligibility:

DecisionTable ApplicantBalanceTransferCreditCardEligibilityDecisionTable				
If	If	If	If	Then
Applicant Sole Annual Income Amount	Applicant Residential Status	Applicant Application Credit Card Previously Applied in Last 6 months	Applicant Number of Years Address History	Applicant Balance Transfer Credit Card Eligibility
>= 10000	UK Resident	FALSE	>= 3	Eligible
< 10000				Ineligible
	Non-UK Resident			Ineligible
		TRUE		Ineligible
			< 3	Ineligible

Fig. 6-3

Any comments here?

READER. This is a single-hit decision table that covers all possible combinations of 4 variables.

DecisionTable ApplicantCreditCardEligibilityDecisionTable		
If	If	Then
Applicant Card Type	Applicant Credit Score	Applicant Credit Card Eligibility
Student	>= 500	Eligible
Student	< 500	Ineligible
Private	>= 750	Eligible
Private	< 750	Ineligible
Balance Transfer	>= 750	${Applicant Balance Transfer Credit Card Eligibility}
Balance Transfer	< 750	Ineligible
		Eligible

Fig. 6-4

AUTHOR. And finally, Fig. 6-4 describes the business logic for the Applicant Credit Card Eligibility. Comments?

READER. This is again a single-hit decision table that uses Applicant Card Type and Applicant Credit Score (calculated by the scorecard on Fig. 6-2). This is certainly a complete decision table as it contains the default value in the last (unconditional) rule that is typical for single-hit decision tables.

AUTHOR. That's right. What will this table produce as Applicant Credit Card Eligibility if the 5th rule is satisfied (Applicant Card Type = Balance Transfer AND Applicant Credit Score >= 750)?

READER. It will produce "Applicant Balance Transfer Credit Card Eligibility"... Wait a minute, it should not be the name of this variable but rather its value calculated in the decision table on Fig. 6-3, right?

AUTHOR. And that's exactly what OpenRules will do. Before considering the content of this cell as just a constant like "Eligible" or "Ineligible", OpenRules will try to interpret it as **a DMN FEEL expression**. It will recognize that Applicant Balance Transfer Credit Card Eligibility is a name of the decision variable defined in the Glossary, and will assign the value of this variable to the conclusion variable "Applicant Credit Card Eligibility".

READER. This is really good and intuitive, and I don't need to specify anything else.

AUTHOR. By the way, you still may explicitly tell OpenRules that you want to take the value of this variable instead of its name. If you write

> ${Applicant Balance Transfer Credit Card Eligibility}
>
> or even
>
> $Applicant Balance Transfer Credit Card Eligibility

OpenRules still will continue to work fine.

OK, it seems to me you feel pretty comfortable with different types of decision tables. I'd still recommend you to do some experiments with the "DecisionCreditCardApplication" project after the end of this session.

READER. I will certainly do.

AUTHOR. Good. Now it's time to move forward to a more complex topic, namely the accumulation of different values relating not to one but to a **collection of objects**.

So far, we considered separate business concepts (objects) and business rules defined on their attributes (sometimes the attributes themselves were arrays). Now I want to show you how to deal with arrays (or lists) of objects. Let's say you need to define business rules for certain groups of employees inside your department or just determine the minimal or maximal salaries for all department employees. It means you need somehow to **iterate through an array** of all employees and check certain conditions against each employee. Usually, in such situations programming languages use different types of loops, and even DMN defines its own loop that may look like "For employee if department <do something>".

READER. So, we cannot avoid programming constructs in these cases, can we?

AUTHOR. Yes, we can. Today you will see how OpenRules avoids the use of explicitly defined loops. Let's specify our business problem in more precise terms and try to build the proper complete decision model. So, let's say we have a department with many employees. The following Datatype table defines Employee:

Datatype Employee	
String	name
int	age
String	gender
String	maritalStatus
int	salary
String	wealthCategory

Fig. 6-5

As we plan to accumulate different characteristics for all employees within a department, I will define the Datatype Department as follows:

Datatype Department	
String	department
Employee[]	employees
int	minSalary
int	maxSalary
int	totalSalary
int	numberOfHighPaidEmployees

Fig. 6-6

READER. Aha, you used Employee[] again with "[]" to specify an array of employees like we previously specified String[] for allergies.

AUTHOR. Exactly. I also want to apply business rules to determine values of minSalary, maxSalary, totalSalary, and the number of high-paid employees within a department.

READER. I understand that it is easy to define a rule for one employee to be considered as "high-paid" by checking if his/her salary is larger than a certain amount. But how will do it for every employee?

AUTHOR. Just be patient – we are getting there. First, let's define out test data. Here is the list of all employees in two departments of our fictitious organization:

Data Employee allEmployees					
name	maritalStatus	gender	age	salary	wealthCategory
Name	Marital Status	Gender	Age	Salary	Wealth Category
Robinson	Married	Female	25	20000	?
Warner	Married	Male	45	150000	?
Stevens	Single	Male	24	35000	?
White	Married	Female	32	75000	?
Smith	Single	Male	46	110000	?
Green	Married	Female	28	40000	?
Brown	Married	Male	32	65000	?
Klaus	Married	Male	54	85000	?
Houston	Single	Female	47	35000	?
Long	Married	Male	29	40000	?
Short	Single	Male	22	20000	?
Doe	Single	Female	21	21000	?

Fig. 6-7

And here are our two departments:

Data Department departments					
department	employees	minSalary	maxSalary	totalSalary	numberOfHighPaidEmployees
	>allEmployees				
Department	Employees	Min Salary	Max Salary	Total Salary	Number Of High-Paid Employees
Department 1	Robinson	0	0	0	0
	Warner				
	Stevens				
	White				
	Smith				
	Green				
Department 2	Brown	0	0	0	0
	Klaus				
	Houston				
	Long				
	Short				
	Doe				

Fig. 6-8

As you can see in Fig. 6-8, we defined two departments. For each department, all employees from the array "allEmployees" are listed in the second column by putting their names in a separate sub-row. To support such references between Data tables, we added **">allEmployees**" in the column "Employees" using an additional row.

READER. I guess all employee names must be unique. I also can see that you merged all sub-rows for other columns within each department's row.

AUTHOR, Yes, it is very important. For example, by merging sub-rows for the row "Department 1" and the column "Min Salary", we explicitly show that this is the minimal salary for the all employees from Robinson to Green in the Department 1.

Now you probably will not have a problem putting together the glossary.

READER. Of course, here is the glossary:

Glossary glossary		
Variable Name	**Business Concept**	**Attribute**
Name	Employee	name
Marital Status		age
Gender		gender
Age		maritalStatus
Salary		salary
Wealth Category		wealthCategory
Department	Department	department
Employees		employees
Min Salary		minSalary
Max Salary		maxSalary
Total Salary		totalSalary
Number Of High-Paid Employees		numberOfHighPaidEmployees

Fig. 6-9

AUTHOR. Good. Now let's try to define high-paid employees. The decision table for one employee may look as follows:

DecisionTableMultiHit EvaluateOneEmployee					
Condition		Conclusion		Conclusion	
Salary		Wealth Category		Number Of High-Paid Employees	
>=	85000	Is	HighPaid	+=	1
<	85000	Is	Regular		

Fig. 6-10

READER. I understand how you defined Wealth Category: "HighPaid" for those who make 85K or more and "Regular" for others. But why did you use the "collect" operator "+=" to define the Number Of High-Paid Employees? Is it similar to what we did for scorecards?

AUTHOR. Yes and No. This operator still tells OpenRules to increment the variable "Number Of High-Paid Employees" by 1. However, each increment will take place, not for different satisfied rules, but rather for each employee for which this decision table will be executed. OpenRules allow us to specify a special action called "ActionRulesOnArray" inside a regular decision table to iterate through an array of objects. Here is such a table:

DecisionTable EvaluateAllEmployees			
Action	ActionRulesOnArray		
Number Of High Paid Employees	Array of Objects	Object Type	Rules
0	Employees	Employee	EvaluateOneEmployee

Fig. 6-11

The first (regular) action will simply initialize the variable "Number Of High-Paid Employees" with 0. The second action will execute our decision table "EvaluateOneEmployee" for every element of the array "Employees" defined in the glossary for our current Department object. To iterate through an array this action-column uses 3 sub-columns for:

1) **Array Of Objects** with the name of the array (e.g. Employees)
2) **Object Type** with the type of the array (e.g. Employee)
3) **Rules** with the name of the decision table that will be executed for each element of the array (e.g. EvaluateOneEmployee).

READER. I think I understand how the decision table "EvaluateAllEmployees" works. We will probably call it from our high-level decision and it will automatically call the decision table "EvaluateOneEmployee" for every employee from the array "Employees" for our business object "Department". That's how the variable "Number Of High-Paid Employees" will be incremented for every department's employee with Salary >= 85000.

AUTHOR. That's a correct explanation. I just want you to understand that this is an OpenRules way to model array iterations without the necessity to use programming loops. However, the decision table in Fig. 6-11 is equivalent to the following Java snippet:

Method void EvaluateAllEmployees(Decision decision)

```
Object[] employees = decision.getObjects("Employees");
for(int i=0; i<employeess.length; i++) {
  decision.useBusinessObject("Employee", employees[i]);
  decision.execute("EvaluateOneEmployee",decision);
}
```

Fig. 6-12

I know that I promised you not to do programming, however for completeness of this guide I wanted to show this special Excel table of the type "Method" that can contain any Java snippet. One day if your logic becomes too cumbersome for a decision table, you might ask your DEVELOPER to help you to create the proper Java method.

READER. OK, I appreciate it, but now I wonder how to determine other aggregated Department attributes: Min Salary, Max Salary, and Total Salary.

AUTHOR. We can just extend our two previous tables. Here is the properly updated table "EvaluateOneEmployee":

DecisionTableMultiHit EvaluateOneEmployee											
Condition		Conclusion		Conclusion		Conclusion		Conclusion		Conclusion	
Salary		Wealth Category		Number Of High-Paid Employees		Total Salary		Max Salary		Min Salary	
>=	85000	Is	HighPaid	+=	1						
<	85000	Is	Regular								
						+=	Salary	Max	Salary	Min	Salary

Fig. 6-13

READER. You've just added 3 more conclusions. The first one will increment the variable "Total Salary" with the Salary of the currently considered employee. You didn't tell me about "Max" and "Min". Are they special operators?

AUTHOR. Exactly! And they are used to define the Maximal/Minimal value of an array's attributes. DMN also uses “>” for the “Max” operator and “<” for the “Min” operator.

READER. I've just noticed that this decision table is multi-hit: otherwise the rule 3 will never be executed.

AUTHOR. Correct. And here is the updated decision table “EvaluateAllEmployees”. It basically remains the same but we simply need to initialize decision variables Min Salary, Max Salary, and Total Salary:

DecisionTable EvaluateAllEmployees						
Action	Action	Action	Action	ActionRulesOnArray		
Min Salary	Max Salary	Total Salary	Number Of High-Paid Employees	Array of Objects	Object Type	Rules
100000	0	0	0	Employees	Employee	EvaluateOneEmployee

Fig. 6-14

READER. I am wondering why MIN Salary is initialized to 100000...

AUTHOR. I've just used a number because it is larger than the salary of at least one employee. The operator “Min” will use this number as a starting point for comparison, and the salary of the very first employee will override this number.

READER. Probably it's safer to make it 1,000,000.

AUTHOR. Probably you are right. Now, let's complete our decision model and try to run it. What are we missing?

READER. We need to define our main decision, but it is really simple. It should just execute one decision table “EvaluateAllEmployees”. So, here it is:

Decision DetermineAggregatedValues	
Decisions	Execute Decision Tables
Evaluate All Department Employees	EvaluateAllEmployees

Fig. 6-15

AUTHOR. We also need to add the table "testCases". Let's start with a test case for one department only and without expected results:

DecisionTableTest testCases	
#	ActionUseObject
Test ID	Department
Test 1	:= departments[0]

Fig. 6-16

READER. OK. Now we should just rename FILE_NAME and DECISION_NAME in the file "define.bat" and we will be able to run our decision model. We can see the first execution results on Fig. 6-17.

AUTHOR. Would you explain this execution protocol?

READER. I will try. First 4 Assign-statements initialize our decision variable in the table "EvaluateAllEmpoyees". Then the line

```
Execute Rules <EvaluateOneEmployee> for a
collection Employees of the type Employee
```

starts our iteration process through the array "Employees".

Dialog-Session 6

```
RUN TEST: Test 1
Decision Run has been initialized
Decision DetermineAggregatedValues: Evaluate All
Department Employees
Assign: Min Salary = 100000 [100000]
Assign: Max Salary = 0 [0]
Assign: Total Salary = 0 [0]
Assign: Number Of High-Paid Employees = 0 [0]
Execute Rules <EvaluateOneEmployee> for a
collection Employees of the type Employee
Conclusion: Wealth Category Is Regular [Regular]
Conclusion: Total Salary += Salary [20000]
Conclusion: Max Salary Max Salary [20000]
Conclusion: Min Salary Min Salary [20000]
Conclusion: Wealth Category Is HighPaid [HighPaid]
Conclusion: Number Of High-Paid Employees += 1 [1]
Conclusion: Total Salary += Salary [170000]
Conclusion: Max Salary Max Salary [150000]
Conclusion: Min Salary Min Salary [20000]
Conclusion: Wealth Category Is Regular [Regular]
Conclusion: Total Salary += Salary [205000]
Conclusion: Max Salary Max Salary [150000]
Conclusion: Min Salary Min Salary [20000]
Conclusion: Wealth Category Is Regular [Regular]
Conclusion: Total Salary += Salary [280000]
Conclusion: Max Salary Max Salary [150000]
Conclusion: Min Salary Min Salary [20000]
Conclusion: Wealth Category Is HighPaid [HighPaid]
Conclusion: Number Of High-Paid Employees += 1 [2]
Conclusion: Total Salary += Salary [390000]
Conclusion: Max Salary Max Salary [150000]
Conclusion: Min Salary Min Salary [20000]
Conclusion: Wealth Category Is Regular [Regular]
Conclusion: Total Salary += Salary [430000]
Conclusion: Max Salary Max Salary [150000]
Conclusion: Min Salary Min Salary [20000]
Decision has been finalized
Validating results for the test <Test 1>
Test 1 was successful
```

Fig. 6-17

We can see 4 conclusions for the first employee:

```
Conclusion: Wealth Category Is Regular [Regular]
Conclusion: Total Salary += Salary [20000]
Conclusion: Max Salary Max Salary [20000]
Conclusion: Min Salary Min Salary [20000]
```

After applying the same "EvaluateOneEmployee" rules to the second employee, we see these 4 lines:

```
Conclusion: Wealth Category Is HighPaid [HighPaid]
Conclusion: Number Of High-Paid Employees += 1 [1]
Conclusion: Total Salary += Salary [170000]
Conclusion: Max Salary Max Salary [150000]
Conclusion: Min Salary Min Salary [20000]
```

We can see how this iteration process continues for all remaining employees.

AUTHOR. Now you can add the second test-case using Department 2, and also you can add expected results using the column "ActionExpect".

READER. How would I know the expected results?

AUTHOR. You can try to calculate them manually. Or if you already trust our decision model, put all zeros instead of the expected results and then use all produced mismatches to modify them.

READER. I got it. Here are my final test-cases:

DecisionTableTest testCases					
#	ActionUseObject	ActionExpect	ActionExpect	ActionExpect	ActionExpect
Test ID	Department	Min Salary	Max Salary	Total Salary	Number Of High-Paid Employees
Test 1	:= departments[0]	20000	150000	430000	2
Test 2	:= departments[1]	20000	85000	266000	1

Fig. 6-18

The new execution protocol now says "All 2 test succeeded!"

AUTHOR. Congratulations! Now, when you almost "touched" a loop (sorry, the decision table with ActionRulesOnArray), I hope you get a better understanding how to deal with collections of objects. We will continue to work with more complex collections next time.

READER. Thank you. I'd not say it was simple, but now I feel more comfortable with those notorious "loops".

Suggested Exercises.

1. Execute and analyze the decision model "DecisionCreditCardApplication". Try to change the scorecard to see how it affects the decision outcome.
2. Enhance the model "DecisionAggregatedValues" by adding and calculating "Total Number of Employees" within one department.
3. Enhance the model "DecisionAggregatedValues" by adding and calculating "Number of Low-Paid Employees".
4. Expand the numbers of departments and employees and test the model again.

5. The execution results are saved in every Department object. Try to display a department within every test-cases and analyze the printed results.
   [Hint: add *:= decision.log($O{Department})* to the main table "DetermineAggregatedValues"]

Dialog-Session 7: Complete Decision Model "Determine Auto Insurance Premium"

Discussed Topics:

- High-Level Decision Requirements Diagram
- Determine Client Eligibility Rating DRD
- Iterating Through Drivers And Cars
- Divide Driver Eligibility Logic Into 4 Pieces
- Driver Contributions To Client Eligibility Score
- Car Contributions To Client Eligibility
- Defining Client Eligibility Rating
- Calculating Client Premium
- Drvie Premium Scorecard
- Car Premium Scorecard
- How to Split Glossary
- Test-Cases and Execution

Related OpenRules Project:

DecisionInsurancePremium

AUTHOR. Today we are going to build and analyze a relatively complex decision model that evaluates client eligibility for auto insurance and if yes calculates the insurance premium. Premium calculation is one of the most popular use of business rules technology. We will follow the problem definition as it was offered in 2005 to different business rules vendors to demonstrate their product's capabilities at the Business Rules Forum (now BBC). This problem was revived in 2015 as a DMCommunity Challenge using the original name "UServ Product Derby". This challenge deals with vehicle insurance problems including eligibility, pricing and cancellation policies for a hypothetical insurance company "UServ".

Dialog-Session 7

READER. I've looked at the problem definition and it seems quite complicated.

AUTHOR. Yes, this is a quite complex problem, but it is good to already have such a detailed description even if it looks long. To simplify our work today we will use the already provided Excel files from the OpenRules project "DecisionInsurance Premium". We will go through every piece of decision logic and will leave no stone unturned. Prepare to be patient - it will be a long session.

READER. OK, I've downloaded all xls-files from this project. Should we begin with the file Decision.xls?

AUTHOR. Yes, and first let's look at the high-level Decision Requirements Diagram (DRD):

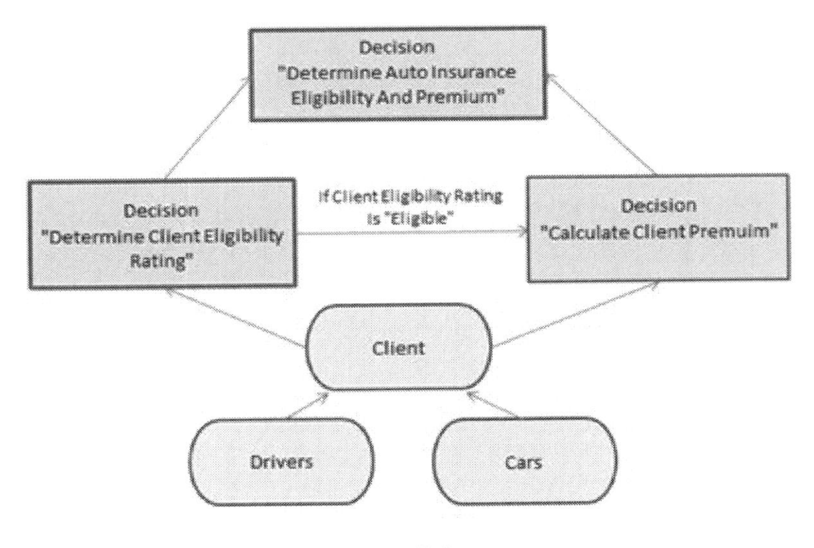

Fig. 7-1

The decision "DetermineAutoInsuranceEligibilityAndPremium" will consist of two major sub-decisions:

1) DetermineClientEligibilityRating
2) CalculateClientPremium

The first decision will define a value of the decision variable "Eligibility Rating" and if it is "Eligible" then the "Client Premium" should be calculated.

READER. Here is the representation of the top-level decision requirement diagram using a table of type "Decision":

Decision DetermineAutoInsuranceEligibilityAndPremium		
Condition		ActionExecute
Client Eligibility Rating		Execute Sub-Decisions
		DetermineClientEligibilityRating
Is	Eligible	CalculateClientPremium

Fig. 7-2

AUTHOR. Note that both the diagram elements and the decision names in this table have associated hyperlinks created using Excel. I recommend using this simple but very useful feature in your own decision modeling practice as well. These hyperlinks serve as a glue between different elements of a decision model.

READER. Yes, using such hyperlinks we may navigate through different Excel files, worksheets, and tables inside our decision model.

AUTHOR. OK. Before we move to the actual business logic, it is important to understand all the business concepts we will be dealing with: Clients, Drivers and Cars. How do you understand them based on the problem description?

READER. I am thinking about the "Client" as a family or a business that needs to insure its multiple cars and drivers. They actually provided examples of such clients, e.g. the Klaus family, in which Sara drives a Honda Odyssey and Spenser drives a Toyota Camry. We will probably need Datatypes "Client", "Car", and "Driver" and the proper Data tables for them.

AUTHOR. Yes, we will look at them later on. For now we will continue our top-down design of the decision model. Splitting one large decision into two smaller sub-decisions allows us to deal with each of them separately (following the design pattern "Divide and Conquer" [3]). Let's look at the DRD for the first sub-decision already prepared by OpenRules using Excel. To keep the DRD relatively simple, I will show only a part of the actual diagram in Fig. 7-3. It covers first two levels of the sub-decision "DetermineClientEligibilityRating":

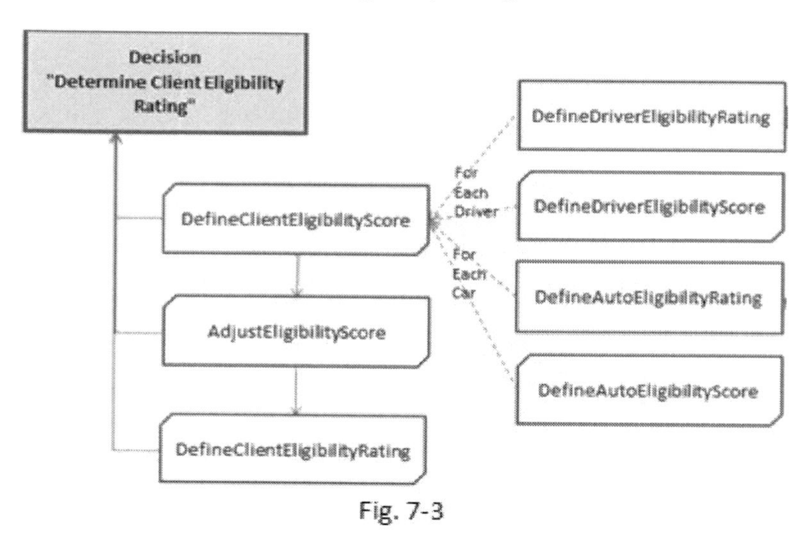

Fig. 7-3

How would you compare this diagram with the problem definition in plain English?

READER. I'd say it is quite close to the plain English. We can see that this sub-decision depends on 3 other components:

- Define Client Eligibility Score
- Adjust Client Eligibility Score
- Define Client Eligibility Rating

It is naturally presented in Fig. 7-4:

Decision DetermineClientEligibilityRating	
Decisions	**Decision Tables**
Define Client Eligibility Score	DefineClientEligibilityScore
Adjust Eligibility Score for prefered and elite clients	AdjustEligibilityScore
Define Client Eligibility Rating	DefineClientEligibilityRating

Fig. 7-4

What really looks quite complex to me is the business logic that specifies Client Eligibility Score as it deals with multiple drivers and multiple cars.

AUTHOR. Yes, and the DRD in Fig. 7-3 reflects this complexity. As you can see, there are two types of business rules:

1) Rules that specify how to calculate eligibility scores for every driver and for every car;
2) Rules that accumulate eligibility scores of ALL drivers and ALL cars in one Client Eligibility Score.

Sound familiar?

READER. When you say "accumulate eligibility scores of ALL drivers" I am thinking about our previous session when we accumulated different values for all employees within one department.

AUTHOR. Exactly! So, the words "For Each Driver" and "For Each Car" in Fig. 7-3 should not confuse you anymore – you already know how to handle such "loops".

READER. There you go again.. but I think this time I understand what you mean.

AUTHOR. In this case you should be able to explain the following decision table that implements the sub-decision "DefineClientEligibilityScore":

DecisionTableMultiHit DefineClientEligibilityScore			
Action	ActionRulesOnArray		
Client Eligibility Score	Array of Objects	Object Type	Rules
0			
	Drivers	Driver	DefineDriverEligibilityRating
	Drivers	Driver	DefineDriverEligibilityScore
	Cars	Car	DefineAutoEligibilityRating
	Cars	Car	DefineAutoEligibilityScore

Fig. 7-5

READER. Let me try. The very first rule simply initializes Client Eligibility Score with zero. The second rule executes the rules "DefineDriverEligibilityRating" for every driver from the array "Drivers". Similarly, the third rule executes the rules "DefineDriverEligibilityScore" for every driver from the array "Drivers". The fourth and the fifth rules executes the rules

"DefineAutoEligibilityRating" and "DefineAutoEligibilityScore" for every car in the array "Cars".

AUTHOR. Right, all these rules will be executed unconditionally one after the other. That's why the type of this decision table is "DecisionTableMultiHit". Now we may concentrate on the rules for one driver and one car without worrying about iterations ("loops").

READER. That's good as these rules should be much easier to specify.

AUTHOR. Yes, click on the hyperlink DefineDriverEligibilityRating in the table 7-5 to open the decision table for one driver.

READER. Here it is:

Decision DefineDriverEligibilityRating	
Decisions	**Decision Tables**
Define Age Category	DefineAgeCategory
Define Training Certification	DefineTrainingCertification
Define Driving Record Category	DefineDrivingRecordCategory
Define Driver Eligibility	DefineDriverEligibility

Fig. 7-6

Basically, we divide and conquer, dividing the decision logic into 4 smaller pieces which can handle different driver's attributes. Let's begin with the calculation logic for Driver Eligibility Rating – the last sub-decision in Fig. 7-6.

DecisionTable DefineDriverEligibility				
Condition		Condition		Action
Driver Age Category		Driver Has Training Certification		Driver Eligibility Rating
Is One Of	Young,Senior	Is	FALSE	Not Eligible
Is One Of	Young,Senior	Is	TRUE	Eligible
				Eligible

Fig. 7-7

This is a straight-forward single-hit decision table, that based on Driver Age Category and Training Certification sets Driver Eligibility Rating as Eligible (the default) or Not Eligible (only for a Young or Senior driver without training certification).

Driver Age Category is defined by this simple decision table:

DecisionTable DefineAgeCategory				
Condition		Condition		Action
Driver Gender		Driver Age		Driver Age Category
Is	Male	Is Less	25	Young
Is	Female	Is Less	20	Young
		Is More Than	70	Senior
				Regular

Fig. 7-8

The variable "Driver Has Training Certification" is defined by another simple decision table:

DecisionTable DefineTrainingCertification							
Condition		Condition		Condition		Conclusion	
Driver has taken training from school		Driver has taken training from a licensed driver training company		Driver has taken a senior citizen driver's refresher course		Driver Has Training Certification	
Is	TRUE					Is	TRUE
		Is	TRUE			Is	TRUE
				Is	TRUE	Is	TRUE
						Is	FALSE

Fig. 7-9

AUTHOR. Yes, each table by itself is very simple. We also need to define Driving Record Category as High Risk or Low Risk. Based on this value different drivers may contribute differently into the calculation of the Client Eligibility Score. Here is the decision table:

DecisionTable DefineDrivingRecordCategory						
Condition		Condition		Condition		Action
Driver has been convicted of a DUI		Number of moving violations in the last two years		Number of accidents		Driving Record Category
Is	TRUE					Hish Risk
		Is More	3			Hish Risk
				Is More	2	Hish Risk
						Low Risk

Fig. 7-10

READER. Probably the designer of this decision model added this table into the decision in Fig. 7-6 not right away but only when he or she really needed to know the value of the variable "Driving Record Category".

AUTHOR. That's probably true. And it only confirms how flexible the selected approach "Divide and Conquer" is. Now we are ready to move to the calculation of Driver Eligibility Score for one driver. Please, click on the hyperlink DefineDriverEligibilityScore in the table 7-5 to open the corresponding decision table.

READER. Here it is:

DecisionTableMultiHit DefineDriverEligibilityScore							
Condition		Condition		Condition		Conclusion	
Driver Age Category		Driver Eligibility Rating		Driving Record Category		Client Eligibility Score	
Is	Young	Is Not	Eligible			+=	30
Is	Senior	Is Not	Eligible			+=	20
				Is	High Risk	+=	100

Fig. 7-11

I'd rather call this decision table "DefineClientEligibilityScore".

AUTHOR. You have a point because this table specifies Client Eligibility Score and not Driver Eligibility Score (such a variable simply does not exist). Probably this decision table should be really called "DefineDriverContributionToClientEligibilityScore".

READER. Yes, I agree, probably it was done to keep the name shorter. OK, we have covered all rules for drivers. Now we need to follow the hyperlinks in Fig. 7-5 for cars. When I clicked on the hyperlink DefineAutoEligibilityRating in table 7-5, I can see the following decision:

Decision DefineAutoEligibilityRating	
Decisions	**Decision Tables**
Define Potential Theft Rating	DefinePotentialTheftRating
Define Potential Occupant Injury Rating	DefinePotentialOccupantInjuryRating
Define Auto Eligibility Rating	DefineAutoEligibility

Fig. 7-12

This decision will execute 3 listed decision tables for every client's car.

AUTHOR. This table as well the 3 other decision tables that it invokes are located in different worksheets of the file "AutomobileEligibility.xls" . Please show each decision table and provide any comments you may have about them.

READER. OK. Here is the table "DefinePotentialTheftRating":

DecisionTableMultiHit DefinePotentialTheftRating							
Condition		Condition		Condition		Conclusion	
Auto is on High Theft Probability List		Auto is Convertible		Auto Price		Auto Potential Theft Rating	
Is	FALSE			Is Less	20000	Is	Low
Is				Within	[20000..45000]	Is	Moderate
Is	TRUE					Is	High
		Is	TRUE			Is	High
				Is More	45000	Is	High

Fig. 7-13

This is a multi-hit decision table. I don't see any default value in the very first row of this table. This is not good. Now I have to determine whether all possible combinations of these 3 conditions are covered, and it is not easy to say for sure.

AUTHOR. You are right and the designer of this decision table is wrong! There should be a default value specified (say as '?') because even if this table works fine for the current set of test-cases, adding more conditions or intervals for Auto Price may lead to serious problems. Why do you think the designer of this table didn't do it?

READER. Probably he or she was lazy or became tired...

AUTHOR. People always try to take shortcuts to avoid complications. While it probably helped him or her to stay focused on the problem definition (that by the way does not mention this issue at all), the future maintenance consequences should not be underestimated. OK, let's proceed but remember this discussion when you design your own decision tables.

READER. I will. Here is "DefinePotentialOccupantInguryRating":

DecisionTableMultiHit DefinePotentialOccupantInjuryRating				
Condition		Condition		Action
Car Features		Auto is Convertible		Potential Occupant Injury Rating
				Extremely High
Include	Driver's air bag			High
Include	Driver's air bag, Front passenger air bag			Moderate
Include	Driver's air bag, Front passenger air bag, Side panel air bags			Low
Does Not Include	Roll bar	Is	TRUE	Extremely High

Fig. 7-14

This is also a multi-hit decision table, but this time the default value is specified in the first rule. And here is the decision table "DefineAutoEligibility":

DecisionTableMultiHit DefineAutoEligibility				
Condition		Condition		Action
Potential Occupant Injury Rating		Auto Potential Theft Rating		Auto Eligibility Rating
				Eligible
Is	High			Provisional
		Is	High	Provisional
Is	Extremely High			Not Eligible

Fig. 7-15

It looks clean and clear to me.

AUTHOR. Good. Now, to finish with car iterations in Fig. 7-5, please click on the hyperlink DefineAutoEligibilityScore.

READER. It opens the file "ClientEligibility.xls" with the following decision table:

DecisionTableMultiHit DefineAutoEligibilityScore			
Condition		Conclusion	
Auto Eligibility Rating		Client Eligibility Score	
Is	Not Eligible	+=	100
Is	Provisional	+=	50
Is	Eligible	+=	0

Fig. 7-16

Again they forgot a default value.

AUTHOR. This time you are not right. This decision defines how an Auto Eligibility Rating for every car contributes to the Client Eligibility Score. There are only 3 rules in this table. For all other car's eligibility ratings there will be no contributions.

READER. My bad. We do have two decision tables in Figures 7-11 and 7-16 that specify how different drivers and cars contribute to Client Eligibility Score. They remind me a scorecard that was split between different decision tables and each of them do not have to be complete.

AUTHOR. Yes, they are partial scorecards. Now, let's look again at our DRD in Fig. 7-4. We've only completed the first sub-decision "DefineClientEligibilityScore" and there are two more sub-decisions. The good news is that that was the most complex decision with various iterations. The remaining sub-decisions are much simpler. Please click on the next hyperlink AdjustClientScore in Fig. 7-4.

READER. It brings us back to the file "ClientEligibility.xls" and displays the following decision table:

DecisionTableMultiHit AdjustEligibilityScore			
Condition		Conclusion	
Client Segment		Client Eligibility Score	
Is	Preferred	-=	50
Is	Elite	-=	100

Fig. 7-17

Oh, this is another partial scorecard that adjusts Client Eligibility Score based on Client Segment. The only noticeable point here is the use of the operator "-=" that contrary to "+=" decrements the score by provided value. Probably I still could use the operator "+=" but with negative values -50 and -100.

AUTHOR. Yes, you can. And now please click on the next hyperlink DefineClientEligibilityRating in Fig. 7-4.

READER. It displays the following decision table:

DecisionTableMultiHit DefineClientEligibilityRating					
Condition		Condition		Conclusion	
Client Eligibility Score		Long Term Client		Client Eligibility Rating	
Is Less	100			Is	Eligible
Within	[100..250]			Is	To be Reviewed
Is More	250			Is	Not Eligible
		Is	TRUE	Is	Eligible

Fig. 7-18

OK, let's see. This is a multi-hit table. Its first 3 mutually-exclusive rules define Client Eligibility Rating based on Client Eligibility Score. The fourth rule may override the previous result when Long Term Client is TRUE. Looks like a very clear decision table to me.

AUTHOR. Good. This table completes the sub-decision "DetermineClientEligibilityRating" by specifying Client Eligibility Rating. According to the high-level decision in Fig. 7-2, if it is "Eligible" we should proceed with the sub-decision "CalculateClientPremium". First. Let's take a look at its DRD presented in the file "Decision.xls". Once again I will show only the first two levels of this DRD:

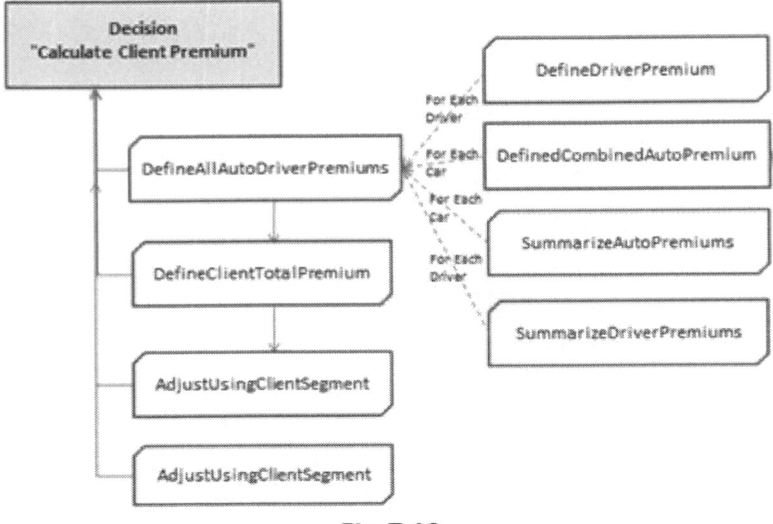

Fig. 7-19

READER. The first sub-decision "DecineAllAutoDriverPremuims" will iterate through all drivers and cars, and will even do it even several times.

AUTHOR. Of course, before calculating Client Total Premium we need to calculate premiums for each driver and each car, and then summarize them in accordance with the business logic specified by the problem description. You need to be patient as we decided to "leave no stone unturned".

READER. OK, let's do it. We need to go through all 4 high-level sub-decisions beginning with "DefineAllAutoDriverPremuims". When I clicked on this hyperlink it opened the file "ClientPremium.xls" and displayed the following decision table:

DecisionTableMultiHit DefineAllAutoDriverPremiums					
Action	Action	Action	ActionRulesOnArray		
Client Driver Premium	Client Base Premium	Client Auto Premium	Array of Objects	Object Type	Rules
0	0	0			
			Drivers	Driver	DefineDriverPremium
			Cars	Car	DefinedCombinedAutoPremium
			Drivers	Driver	SummarizeDriverPremiums
			Cars	Car	SummarizeAutoPremiums

Fig. 7-20

It's quite similar to the table in Fig. 7-5. The first rule initializes 3 premium variables:

- Client Driver Premium
- Client Base Premium
- Client Auto Premium.

Then it executes our 4 "loops" going (twice!) through each driver and each car.

AUTHOR. I see you do not have problems with loops anymore. Let's quickly go through the decision tables.

READER. Here is the first decision table that will be executed for each driver:

DecisionTableMultiHit DefineDriverPremium									
Condition		Condition		Condition		Condition		Conclusion	
Driver Age Category		Marital Status		State		Driving Record Category		Driver Premium	
								=	0
Is	Young	Is	Married	Is One Of	CA,NY,VA			+=	700
Is		Is	Single					+=	720
Is		Is	Married	Is Not One Of	CA,NY,VA			+=	300
Is		Is	Single					+=	300
Is	Senior			Is One Of	CA,NY,VA			+=	500
Is	Senior			Is Not One Of	CA,NY,VA			+=	200
						Is	High Risk	+=	1000
								+=	Number of accidents * 150

Fig. 7-21

So, this multi-hit table is a typical scorecard -- just in this case they use Driver Premium as a score.

AUTHOR. Pay attention to the use of operators "Is One Of" and "Is Not One Of" with lists of states.

READER. Yes, it's quite intuitive – we've already discussed them in previous sessions. Here is the second sub-decision:

Decision DefinedCombinedAutoPremium	
Decisions	Decision Tables
Define Auto Premium	DefineAutoPremium
Define Auto Discount	DefineAutoDiscount
Apply Auto Discounts	ApplyAutoDiscount

Fig. 7-22

To calculate Combined Auto Premium, it invokes 3 its own sub-decisions. Here is the first one "DefineAutoPremium":

DecisionTableMultiHit DefineAutoPremium																	
Condition		Condition		Condition		Condition		Condition		Condition		Condition		Conclusion		Conclusion	
Car Type		Car is New		Car Age		Uninsured motorist coverage is included		Medical coverage is included		Potential Occupant Injury Rating		Auto Potential Theft Rating		Auto Premium		Base Premium	
														=	0	=	0
Is	Compact													+=	250	+=	250
Is	Sedan													+=	400	+=	400
Is	Luxury													+=	500	+=	500
		Is	TRUE											+=	400		
		Is	FALSE	Is Less	5									+=	300		
				Within	[5..10]									+=	250		
						Is	TRUE							+=	300		
								Is	TRUE					+=	600		
										Is	Extremely High			+=	1000		
										Is	High			+=	500		
												Is	High	+=	500		

Fig. 7-23

It is difficult to see this table as it has 7 conditions and 2 conclusions.

AUTHOR. We can open this decision table directly from the Excel file "AutomobilePremium.xls". Again, it is a typical scorecard: the only special feature is the calculation of two different scores (Auto Premium and Base Premium) in one table. Let's proceed to "DefineAutoDiscount".

READER. Here it goes – see Fig. 7-24. This is simply another scorecard, this time for Auto Discount Percentage.

DecisionTableMultiHit DefineAutoDiscount					
Condition		Condition		Conclusion	
Car Features		Auto Potential Theft Rating		Auto Discount Percentage	
				=	0
Include	Driver's air bag			+=	12
Include	Driver's air bag, Front passenger air bag			+=	3
Include	Driver's air bag, Front passenger air bag, Side panel air bags			+=	3
Include	Alarm sysytem	Is	High	+=	10

Fig. 7-24

And finally, I will click on the hyperlink "ApplyAutoDiscount":

DecisionTableMultiHit ApplyAutoDiscount	
Conclusion	
Auto Premium	
Is	Auto Premium * (100 - Auto Discount Percentage) / 100

Fig. 7-25

Aha, this is a nice formula that calculates Auto Premium using a DMN FEEL expression.

AUTHOR. Yes, this decision model gives us good examples of different DMN constructs. So, we completed the second set of rules from the table in Fig. 7-20. Now let's proceed to the third one.

READER. From this table I will click on the hyperlink "SummarizeDriverPremiums". It displays this very simple decision table:

DecisionTableMultiHit SummarizeDriverPremiums	
Conclusion	
Client Driver Premium	
+=	Driver Premium

Fig. 7-26

Basically, it accumulates all driver's premium as Client Driver Premium. It is similar to what we did when we calculated Total Salary for all employees. And now let's open the decision table "SummarizeAutoPremiums":

DecisionTableMultiHit SummarizeAutoPremiums			
Conclusion		Conclusion	
Client Auto Premium		Client Base Premium	
+=	Auto Premium	+=	Base Premium

Fig. 7-27

Each of its conclusions accumulates the premiums for all cars (autos).

AUTHOR. Let me continue with the remaining 3 sub-decisions of the diagram in Fig. 7-20. Here is its tabular representation:

Decision CalculateClientPremium	
Decisions	Decision Tables
Define All Premiums for all cars and all drivers	DefineAllAutoDriverPremiums
Define Client Total Premium	DefineClientTotalPremium
Adjust Using Client Segment	AdjustUsingClientSegment
Adjust Using Base Premium	AdjustUsingBasePremium

Fig. 7-28

I will double-click on the link "DefineClientTotalPremium":

DecisionTable DefineClientTotalPremium
Action
Client Total Premium
Client Auto Premium + Client Driver Premium

Fig. 7-29

It is again a straight-forward formula that calculates Client Total Premium as the sum of Client Auto Premium and Client Driver Premium. The only difference with the formula on Fig. 7-25 above is that here instead of Conclusion with two sub-columns we use Action. In both cases we use FEEL expressions.

Now I will double-click on the link "AdjustUsingClientSegment":

DecisionTableMultiHit AdjustUsingClientSegment			
Condition		Conclusion	
Client Segment		**Client Total Premium**	
Is	Preferred	:=	250
Is	Elite	:=	500

Fig. 7-30

It is another simple scorecard. Now I will double-click on the link "AdjustUsingBasePremium":

DecisionTable AdjustUsingBasePremium				
ConditionRealOperReal			Conclusion	
Var <oper> Var			**Client Total Premium**	
Client Total Premium	<	Client Base Premium	=	Client Base Premium

Fig. 7-31

This decision table utilizes a new type of condition called "ConditionRealOperReal" that allows you to specify a condition between two real variables using comparison operators <, >, <=, >=, =. As you may probably guess, this table states:

IF Client Total Premium < Client Base Premium
THEN Client Total Premium = Client Base Premium

I believe we've finally covered the entire business logic of this complex enough decision model.

READER. As we used many different Excel files, can we look at the entire structure of the Rule Repository?

AUTHOR. I am glad that you asked that question. Here it is:

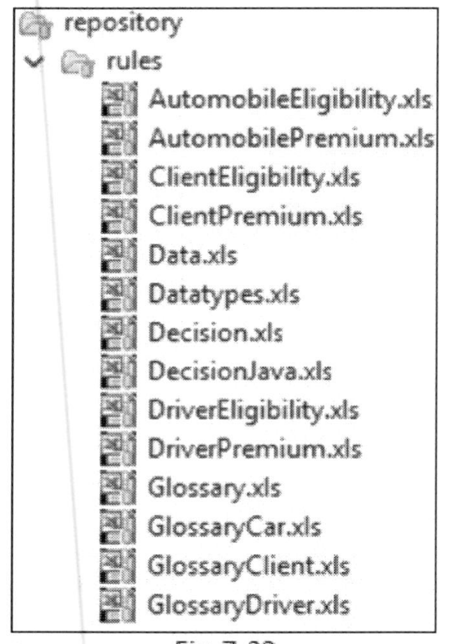

Fig. 7-32

You may see different xls-files being placed in the folder "rules". I'd recommend that you use different sub-folders for each different type of files in your decision models.

READER. I suspect our own decision model will be even more complex. Now we should look at Datatypes, Data, and Glossary. Why do you have 4 different files for a glossary?

AUTHOR. Because sometimes your glossary becomes too big and instead of keeping all business concepts in one big table you may prefer to split it into multiple, smaller glossaries. Let me first open the file "GlossaryClient.xls":

Glossary glossaryClient		
Variable Name	Business Concept	Attribute
Drivers	Client	drivers
Cars		cars
Client Driver Premium		driverPremium
Client Base Premium		basePremium
Client Auto Premium		autoPremium
Client Total Premium		totalPremium
Client Eligibility Score		eligibilityScore
Client Eligibility Rating		eligibilityRating
Long Term Client		longTermClient
Client Segment		segment

Fig. 7-33

Along with regular client attributes it contains two arrays: "Drivers" and "Cars".

Now let's open files "GlossaryCar.xls" and "GlossaryDriver.xls":

Glossary glossaryCar		
Variable Name	**Business Concept**	**Attribute**
Name	Car	name
Year		year
Auto Price		price
Auto is Convertible		convertible
Auto is on High Theft Probability List		onTheTheftProbabilityList
Auto Potential Theft Rating		potentialTheftRating
Car is New		newCar
Car Age		age
Car Features		features
Uninsured motorist coverage is included		uninsuredMotoristCoverageIncluded
Medical coverage is included		medicalCoverageIncluded
Potential Occupant Injury Rating		potentialOccupantInjuryRating
Auto Eligibility Rating		eligibilityRating
Base Premium		basePremium
Auto Discount Percentage		autoDiscount
Auto Premium		autoPremium
Car Type		type

Fig. 7-34

Glossary glossaryDriver		
Variable Name	**Business Concept**	**Attribute**
Name	Driver	name
Driver Gender		gender
Marital Status		maritalStatus
State		state
Driver Age		age
Driver Age Category		ageCategory
Driver Eligibility Rating		eligibilityRating
Driver has been convicted of a DUI		convictedOfDUI
Number of moving violations in the last two years		movingViolationsInLastTwoYears
Number of accidents		numberOfAccidents
Driver has taken training from school		hasTakenTrainingFromSchool
Driver has taken training from a licensed driver training company		hasTakenTrainingFromLicensedDriverTrainingCompany
Driver has taken a senior citizen driver's refresher course		hasTakenSeniorCitizenDriverRefresherCourse
Driver Has Training Certification		hasTrainingCertification
Driver Premium		driverPremium
Driving Record Category		drivingRecordCategory

Fig. 7-35

Now let's look at the file "Glossary.xls":

Method void glossary(Decision decision)

glossaryCar(decision);
glossaryDriver(decision);
glossaryClient(decision);

Fig. 7-36

This is how a split can be done. Instead of one table of the type "Glossary" we use this table of the type "Method" but with the same standard name "glossary". It combines 3 previous glossary tables: glossaryCar, glossaryDriver, and glossaryClient.

READER. I will remember that we always can split large glossaries into several small ones.

AUTHOR. And now let's look at Datatype tables:

Datatype Client	
String	name
Driver[]	drivers
Car[]	cars
double	autoPremium
double	driverPremium
double	basePremium
double	totalPremium
int	eligibilityScore
String	eligibilityRating
boolean	longTermClient
String	segment

Fig. 7-37

Datatype Car	
String	name
int	year
int	price
boolean	newCar
boolean	autoPrenewCarmium
int	age
boolean	convertible
boolean	onTheTheftProbabilityList
String	type
String[]	features
boolean	uninsuredMotoristCoverageIncluded
boolean	medicalCoverageIncluded
String	potentialOccupantInjuryRating
String	eligibilityRating
String	potentialTheftRating
double	basePremium
double	autoDiscount
double	autoPremium

Fig. 7-38

Datatype Driver	
String	name
int	age
String	gender
String	maritalStatus
String	state
String	ageCategory
String	eligibilityRating
boolean	convictedOfDUI
int	movingViolationsInLastTwoYears
int	numberOfAccidents
boolean	hasTakenTrainingFromSchool
boolean	hasTakenTrainingFromLicensedDriverTrainingCompany
boolean	hasTakenSeniorCitizenDriverRefresherCourse
boolean	hasTrainingCertification
String	drivingRecordCategory
double	driverPremium

Fig. 7-39

Note that the datatype "Client" in Fig. 7-37 defines "drivers" and "cars" as arrays.

Now I will open the test-objects: "drivers", "cars", and "clients" located in the file "Data.xls". Here are our drivers:

Data Driver drivers								
name	**Name**	Sara Klaus	Spenser Klaus	Mark Houston	Angie Houston	Ray Meno	Shane Meno
gender	**Driver Gender**	Female	Male	Male	Female	Male	Male
maritalStatus	**Marital Status**	Single	Single	Single	Single	Married	Single
state	**State**	AR	AR	AR	AR	CA	CA
age	**Driver Age**	38	17	38	17	45	21
ageCategory	**Driver Age Category**	?	?	?	?	45	?
eligibilityRating	**Driver Eligibility Rating**	?	?	?	?	?	?
convictedOfDUI	**Driver has been convicted of a DUI**	FALSE	FALSE	FALSE	FALSE	FALSE	FALSE
movingViolationsInLastTwoYears	**Number of moving violations in the last two years**	0	0	1	0	1	3
numberOfAccidents	**Number of accidents**	0	0	0	0	0	2
hasTakenTrainingFromSchool	**Driver has taken training from school**	FALSE	TRUE	FALSE	TRUE	FALSE	TRUE
hasTakenTrainingFromLicensedDriverTrainingCompany	**Driver has taken training from a licensed driver training company**	FALSE	FALSE	FALSE	FALSE	FALSE	FALSE
hasTakenSeniorCitizenDriverRefresherCourse	**Driver has taken a senior citizen driver's refresher course**	FALSE	FALSE	FALSE	FALSE	FALSE	FALSE
hasTrainingCertification	**Driver Has Training Certification**	?	?	?	?	?	?
drivingRecordCategory	**Driving Record Category**	?	?	?	?	?	?
driverPremium	**Driver Premium**	0	0	0	0	0	0

Fig. 7-40

In this case the table of the type "Data" presents different drivers in columns while previously the data elements were presented in rows. Both representations are equivalent, just this time the "vertical" representation is more convenient for display purposes.

Here are our cars:

Data Car cars				
name	Name	Honda Odyssey	Toyota Camry	VW Bug
year	Year	2005	2002	1965
price	Auto Price	39000	12000	1500
convertible	Auto is Convertible	FALSE	FALSE	TRUE
newCar	Car is New	FALSE	FALSE	FALSE
age	Car Age	1	4	42
onTheTheftProbabilityList	Auto is on High Theft Probability List	FALSE	FALSE	TRUE
type	Car Type	Luxury	Compact	Compact
features	Car Features	Driver's air bag	Driver's air bag	Driver's air bag
		Front passenger air bag	Front passenger air bag	Front passenger air bag
		Side panel air bags		
		Alarm system		
uninsuredMotoristCoverageIncluded	Uninsured Motorist Coverage Is Included	TRUE	TRUE	TRUE
medicalCoverageIncluded	Medical Coverage Is Included	TRUE	TRUE	TRUE
potentialOccupantInjuryRating	Potential Occupant Injury Rating	?	?	?
eligibilityRating	Auto Eligibility Rating	?	?	?
potentialTheftRating	Auto Potential Theft Rating	?	?	?
basePremium	Base Premium	0	0	0
autoDiscount	Auto Discount Percent	0	0	0
autoPremium	Auto Premium	0	0	0

Fig. 7-41

This is also a vertical Data table that includes 3 cars. These cars will be assigned to different drivers from the table 7-40 in the following table "clients":

Data Client clients								
name		Name	Client 1		Client 2		Client 3	
drivers	>drivers	Drivers	Sara Klaus	Spenser Klaus	Mark Houston	Angie Houston	Ray Meno	Shane Meno
cars	>cars	Cars	Honda Odyssey	Toyota Camry	Honda Odysse	Toyota Camry	Honda Odyssey	VW Bug
autoPremium		Client Auto Premium	0	0	0	0	0	0
driverPremium		Client Driver Premium	0	0	0	0	0	0
basePremium		Client Base Pemium	0	0	0	0	0	0
autoPremium		Client Auto Pemium	0	0	0	0	0	0
totalPremium		Client Total Premium	0	0	0	0	0	0
eligibilityScore		Client Eligibility Score	0	0	0	0	0	0
eligibilityRating		Client Eligibility Rating	?	?	?	?	?	?
longTermClient		Long Term Client	FALSE	FALSE	FALSE	FALSE	FALSE	FALSE
segment		Client Segment	Preferred	Preferred	Regular	Regular	Elite	Elite

Fig. 7-42

READER. I can see that references like “>drivers” and “>cars” are used here again in the row Drivers and Cars. I remember from the last session that they allow us to refer to the proper driver and car by simply using their names.

AUTHOR. Very good. And finally, here is the table that defines our test-cases with expected results:

DecisionTableTest testCases				
#	ActionUseObject	ActionExpect	ActionExpect	ActionExpect
Test ID	Client	Client Driver Premium	Client Auto Premium	Client Total Premium
Test 1	:= clients[0]	300.00	2626.50	2676.50
Test 2	:= clients[1]	300.00	2626.50	2926.50
Test 3	:= clients[2]	1020.00	3646.50	4166.50

Fig. 7-43

Dialog-Session 7

READER. After all these preparations and thorough analysis, I expect we can run this decision model against these test-cases. First, let me check what is inside the file "define.bat":

```
set FILE_NAME=repository/rules/Decision.xls
set DECISION_NAME=DetermineAutoInsuranceEligibilityAndPremium
```

Aha, FILE_NAME refers to our main file Decision.xls and DECISION_NAME refers to our main decision in Fig. 7-2.

Now I can double-click on "run.bat" to run our decision model.

AUTHOR. Good job – the final statement is "`All 3 tests succeeded!`" I am afraid the produced execution protocol is too long to be reproduced. Let's just show the execution results for the third test-case. I highlighted the key sub-decisions:

`RUN TEST: Test 3`

`Decision Run has been initialized`

`Decision DetermineClientEligibilityRating: Define Client Eligibility Score`

`Assign: Client Eligibility Score = 0 [0]`

`Execute Rules <DefineDriverEligibilityRating> for a collection Drivers of the type Driver`

`Decision DefineDriverEligibilityRating: Define Age Category`

`Assign: Driver Age Category = Regular [Regular]`

`Decision DefineDriverEligibilityRating: Define Training Certification`

`Conclusion: Driver Has Training Certification Is false [false]`

`Decision DefineDriverEligibilityRating: Define Driving Record Category`

`Assign: Driving Record Category = Low Risk [Low Risk]`

`Decision DefineDriverEligibilityRating: Define Driver Eligibility`

Dialog-Session 7

```
Assign: Driver Eligibility Rating = Eligible [Eligible]

Decision DefineDriverEligibilityRating: Define Age Category

Assign: Driver Age Category = Young [Young]

Decision DefineDriverEligibilityRating: Define Training
Certification

Conclusion: Driver Has Training Certification Is true [true]

Decision DefineDriverEligibilityRating: Define Driving Record
Category

Assign: Driving Record Category = Low Risk [Low Risk]

Decision DefineDriverEligibilityRating: Define Driver Eligibility

Assign: Driver Eligibility Rating = Eligible [Eligible]

Execute Rules <DefineDriverEligibilityScore> for a collection
Drivers of the type Driver

Execute Rules <DefineAutoEligibilityRating> for a collection Cars
of the type Car

Decision DefineAutoEligibilityRating: Define Potential Theft
Rating
Conclusion: Auto Potential Theft Rating Is Moderate [Moderate]
Decision DefineAutoEligibilityRating: Define Potential Occupant
Injury Rating
Assign: Potential Occupant Injury Rating = Extremely High
[Extremely High]
Assign: Potential Occupant Injury Rating = High [High]
Assign: Potential Occupant Injury Rating = Moderate [Moderate]
Assign: Potential Occupant Injury Rating = Low [Low]
Decision DefineAutoEligibilityRating: Define Auto Eligibility
Rating
Assign: Auto Eligibility Rating = Eligible [Eligible]
Decision DefineAutoEligibilityRating: Define Potential Theft
Rating
Conclusion: Auto Potential Theft Rating Is High [High]
Conclusion: Auto Potential Theft Rating Is High [High]
Decision DefineAutoEligibilityRating: Define Potential Occupant
Injury Rating
Assign: Potential Occupant Injury Rating = Extremely High
[Extremely High]
Assign: Potential Occupant Injury Rating = High [High]
Assign: Potential Occupant Injury Rating = Moderate [Moderate]
Assign: Potential Occupant Injury Rating = Extremely High
[Extremely High]
```

```
Decision DefineAutoEligibilityRating: Define Auto Eligibility
Rating
Assign: Auto Eligibility Rating = Eligible [Eligible]
Assign: Auto Eligibility Rating = Provisional [Provisional]
Assign: Auto Eligibility Rating = Not Eligible [Not Eligible]
Execute Rules <DefineAutoEligibilityScore> for a collection Cars
of the type Car
Conclusion: Client Eligibility Score += 0 [0]
Conclusion: Client Eligibility Score += 100 [100]
Decision DetermineClientEligibilityRating: Adjust Eligibility
Score for prefered and elite clients
Conclusion: Client Eligibility Score -= 100 [0]
Decision DetermineClientEligibilityRating: Define Client
Eligibility Rating
Conclusion: Client Eligibility Rating Is Eligible [Eligible]
```

Decision CalculateClientPremium: Define All Premiums for all cars and all drivers

```
Assign: Client Driver Premium = 0 [0.0]
Assign: Client Base Premium = 0 [0.0]
Assign: Client Auto Premium = 0 [0.0]
Execute Rules <DefineDriverPremium> for a collection Drivers of
the type Driver
Conclusion: Driver Premium = 0 [0.0]
Conclusion: Driver Premium += Number of accidents * 150 [0.0]
Conclusion: Driver Premium = 0 [0.0]
Conclusion: Driver Premium += 720 [720.0]
Conclusion: Driver Premium += Number of accidents * 150 [1020.0]
Execute Rules <DefinedCombinedAutoPremium> for a collection Cars
of the type Car
Decision DefinedCombinedAutoPremium: Define Auto Premium
Conclusion: Auto Premium = 0 [0.0]
Conclusion: Base Premium = 0 [0.0]
Conclusion: Auto Premium += 500 [500.0]
Conclusion: Base Premium += 500 [500.0]
Conclusion: Auto Premium += 300 [800.0]
Conclusion: Auto Premium += 300 [1100.0]
Conclusion: Auto Premium += 600 [1700.0]
Decision DefinedCombinedAutoPremium: Define Auto Discount
Conclusion: Auto Discount Percentage = 0 [0.0]
Conclusion: Auto Discount Percentage += 12 [12.0]
Conclusion: Auto Discount Percentage += 3 [15.0]
Conclusion: Auto Discount Percentage += 3 [18.0]
Decision DefinedCombinedAutoPremium: Apply Auto Discounts
Conclusion: Auto Premium Is Auto Premium * (100 - Auto Discount
Percentage) / 100 [1394.0]
Decision DefinedCombinedAutoPremium: Define Auto Premium
Conclusion: Auto Premium = 0 [0.0]
Conclusion: Base Premium = 0 [0.0]
Conclusion: Auto Premium += 250 [250.0]
Conclusion: Base Premium += 250 [250.0]
Conclusion: Auto Premium += 300 [550.0]
Conclusion: Auto Premium += 600 [1150.0]
```

```
Conclusion: Auto Premium += 1000 [2150.0]
Conclusion: Auto Premium += 500 [2650.0]
Decision DefinedCombinedAutoPremium: Define Auto Discount
Conclusion: Auto Discount Percentage = 0 [0.0]
Conclusion: Auto Discount Percentage += 12 [12.0]
Conclusion: Auto Discount Percentage += 3 [15.0]
Decision DefinedCombinedAutoPremium: Apply Auto Discounts
Conclusion: Auto Premium Is Auto Premium * (100 - Auto Discount
Percentage) / 100 [2252.5]
Execute Rules <SummarizeDriverPremiums> for a collection Drivers
of the type Driver
Conclusion: Client Driver Premium += Driver Premium [0.0]
Conclusion: Client Driver Premium += Driver Premium [1020.0]
Execute Rules <SummarizeAutoPremiums> for a collection Cars of
the type Car
Conclusion: Client Auto Premium += Auto Premium [1394.0]
Conclusion: Client Base Premium += Base Premium [500.0]
Conclusion: Client Auto Premium += Auto Premium [3646.5]
Conclusion: Client Base Premium += Base Premium [750.0]
Decision CalculateClientPremium: Define Client Total Premium
Assign: Client Total Premium = Client Auto Premium + Client
Driver Premium [4666.5]
Decision CalculateClientPremium: Adjust Using Client Segment
Conclusion: Client Total Premium -= 500 [4166.5]
Decision CalculateClientPremium: Adjust Using Base Premium
Decision has been finalized
Validating results for the test <Test 3>
Test 3 was successful
All 3 tests succeeded!
```

AUTHOR. Please analyze this protocol later on. This was a long, but good exercise as for the first time we've walked through the complex decision model. What is your general impression?

READER. I would say that almost all separate decision elements such as decisions and sub-decisions, decision tables, glossaries, and test-cases look quite clear and intuitive enough. However, it is much more difficult to keep the whole decision model together.

AUTHOR. Yes, real-world decision modeling is not simple and the use of diagrams, hyperlinks, and design patterns such as "Divide and Conquer" or "Scorecards" is really important. Hopefully, your patience during this long dialog-session will be awarded down the road when you develop your own decision models. If you have any problems, you always may contact support@openrules.com for help. Good luck!

Suggested Exercises.

1. Add one more test-case when a client is not eligible for the insurance. Analyze the produced results.
2. The chapter 11 of the DMN Specification includes an example of the decision model for a loan origination process. Its OpenRules-based implementation can be found in the project "DecisionLoanOrigination". Download, analyze, and execute this decision model.
3. Start implementing your own decision models.

References

1. Standard "Decision Model and Notation (DMN)", Object Management Group
2. Real-World Decision Modeling with DMN by James Taylor and Jan Purchase, 2016
3. DMN Method and Style: The Practitioner's Guide to Decision Modeling with Business Rules by Bruce Silver, 2016
4. Knowledge Automation: How to Implement Decision Management in Business Processes by Alan N. Fish, 2012
5. OpenRules, Open Source Business Rules and Decision Management System, http://openrules.com
6. Catalog of DMN Supporting Tools http://openjvm.jvmhost.net/DMNtools/
7. The Decision Model by Barbara von Halle, Larry Goldberg, 2010
8. The History of Modeling Decisions using Tables by Jan Vanthienen, 2012

Printed in Great Britain
by Amazon